GreenSpirit b

CW00403753

Deep green living

Edited by

Marian Van Eyk McCain

With contributions by
Eric Alan, Ted Carter, Helen Cockburn, Rachel Corby,
Duane Elgin, Ellen Gunter, Chris Holmes, Donna Ladkin,
Nigel Lees, Sky McCain, Eleanor O'Hanlon, Peter Quince
and Marianne Worley

Published by GreenSpirit
137 Ham Park Road, London E7 9LE
www.greenspirit.org.uk

Registered Charity No. 1045532

© Marian Van Eyk McCain 2016
First published in the GreenSpirit ebook series in 2016

ISBN 978-0-9935983-7-1

All rights reserved. Except for brief quotations in critical articles or reviews, no part of this book may be reproduced in any manner without prior written permission from the authors.

Design and artwork by Stephen Wollaston (aka Santoshan)
Printed by CreateSpace and Amazon

Cover illustration: Tree © Mariya Ermolaeva/Shutterstock.com
with Sun and Sky by Stephen Wollaston

Page 15 illustration © Lightspring/Shutterstock.com
Page 49 photo © Serif Image Collection 6
Page 99 photo © Serif Image Collection 3
Page 117 photo © Scanrail1/Shutterstock.com
Page 155 © Vanessa Clark 2015

DEEP GREEN LIVING

CONTENTS

INTRODUCTION

I f you are looking at this book, you are probably someone deeply interested in environmental issues. You may be surrounded by other people – friends, family, neighbours and acquaintances – who are also quite 'green' in their ideas and habits. Or you may not be. If you are not, you are probably keenly aware of it and wish you had more like-minded people around you.

There was a time, not so long ago, when being 'green' could be hazardous, especially in certain settings. Even in the early 1990s when I was living in rural Australia I remember feeling decidedly nervous the day I parked my Volvo with its rainbow-coloured Greenpeace bumper sticker immediately downhill of a truck with a bumper sticker that read: *"Save the earth. Doze in a greenie."* And right now, here in my English village, there are locals campaigning vigorously to prevent the erection of wind turbines. But with climate change looming large and an ever-growing awareness of the environmental destruction that our species has wrought, most people these days make at least a token effort to be green. Even the anti-turbine folks almost certainly use their kerbside recycling bins.

In 1999, sociologist Paul H. Ray and psychologist Sherry Ruth Anderson published their book: *The Cultural Creatives. How 50 Million People Are Changing the World* (NY, Three Rivers Press, 2000). Based on extensive research, it was an attempt to reveal just how many people in the Western world really do care about important issues such as environmental destruction and social justice (and that was before we even realized the full extent of climate change). Their results were surprising–and somewhat heartening. You are likely to be a Cultural Creative, they explained, if you...

1. love Nature and are deeply concerned about its destruction
2. are strongly aware of the problems of the whole planet (climate change, destruction of rainforests, overpopulation, lack of ecological sustainability, exploitation of people in poorer countries) and want to see more action on them, such as limiting economic growth
3. would pay more taxes or pay more for consumer goods if you could know the money would go to clean up the environment and to stop global warming
4. place a great deal of importance on developing and maintaining your relationships
5. place a lot of value on helping other people and bringing out their unique gifts
6. do volunteering for one or more good causes
7. care intensely about both psychological and spiritual development
8. see spirituality or religion as important in your life, but are concerned about the role of the Religious Right in politics
9. want more equality for women at work, and more women leaders in business and politics
10. are concerned about violence and abuse of women and children around the world
11. want our politics and government spending to put more emphasis on children's education and well-being, on rebuilding our neighbourhoods and communities, and on creating an ecologically sustainable future
12. are unhappy with both the Left and the Right in politics, and want a to find a new way that is not in the mushy middle
13. tend to be somewhat optimistic about our future, and distrust the cynical and pessimistic view that is given by the media
14. want to be involved in creating a new and better way of life in your country

15. are concerned about what the big corporations are doing in the name of making more profits: downsizing, creating environmental problems, and exploiting poorer countries

16. have your finances and spending under control, and are not concerned about overspending

17. dislike all the emphasis in modern culture on success and 'making it,' on getting and spending, on wealth and luxury goods

18. like people and places that are exotic and foreign, and like experiencing and learning about other ways of life

If you thought about these questions in relation to yourself and answered "yes" to ten or more of them, you are likely to be one of this huge, hidden band of people who are trying to create a peaceful, sustainable world instead of the tumultuous, dangerous, inequitable, unstable and unsustainable one we currently have.

Ray and Anderson estimated that by the year 2000, Cultural Creatives already numbered around fifty million in North America – which is about a quarter of the adult population – and eighty to ninety million in the European Union. That's a huge, invisible, world-wide swell. Later surveys have shown that the numbers continue to rise. So how can it be that there is a group this big and yet nobody seems to have recognised it till now? Well partly because the mainstream media are slaves to the consumer culture and the corporations that profit from it, and it is from the media that we tend to form our impressions of the societies we live in. But partly because this movement – if one can call it that – has not yet fully recognised itself.

What emerged from this study was a realisation that the people we now recognise as Cultural Creatives did not just pop up like mushrooms overnight. They have actually been here all along. It is simply that they have each been busily focusing on the issue which matters to them the most, be it nutrition, health care, spiritual growth, alternative education, the peace movement, the environment, feminism, animal rights, social justice... or whatever.

Economist, environmentalist and social activist Paul Hawken spent over a decade researching organizations dedicated to restoring the environment and fostering social justice. He discovered that from billion-dollar nonprofits to single-person dot.causes, these groups collectively comprise the largest movement on Earth, a movement that has no name, leader, or location, and that has gone largely ignored by politicians and the media. Like Nature itself, it is organizing from the bottom up, in every city, town, and culture and is emerging to be an extraordinary and creative expression of people's needs worldwide. Hawken's research led to the publication of his book *Blessed Unrest: How the Largest Movement in the World Came into Being and Why No One Saw it Coming* (Viking Press 2007).

What we are seeing now, therefore, is a picture of the convergence of many movements, coming together in the same way that streams converge to create rivers.

This coalescence, of course, was inevitable. It is finally dawning on us, in this twenty-first century, that there can be no good health without better education, nor vice versa. It has become obvious that globalisation, multinationals, the rise of supermarkets, junk food, obesity, the widening poverty gap, climate change, degraded topsoil, acidified oceans, animals going extinct, and farmers committing suicide, are all faces of the same monster. We are realising that patriarchal, 'dominator' values harm both women and the Earth, that love of money really is the root of all evil and that peace, social justice and environmental issues are so intertwined that they cannot be disentangled. Above all, we are seeing clearly that a total change in consciousness is imperative. All issues are really one issue. The truth facing us is that human beings must either find new ways to live together sustainably and in harmony on this planet, within the limits of its ability to support us and with deep respect for its natural systems, or we shall all perish – and take most other life forms with us. So those single-issue streams are now becoming a wide, deep river. Either we must all work together to find solutions, to create a new paradigm, a new culture, a new way out of the morass, or the game is up. The planet will survive, even though it may well end up as dry and barren as Mars, but we certainly shan't and neither will most of the other organisms that make up our living world.

Defining ourselves as Cultural Creatives does not mean that we swap all our lapel pins and membership cards for one big, new one. It means that we keep on doing exactly what we are doing, each in his or her own way, to try and make the world a better place. Just as it took many different craftspeople, many talents, many activities to build one of those magnificent, Gothic cathedrals, we each play a unique part in the creation of a new whole.

However, beyond whatever else we do in an organised, social way, the most important thing we can do to further this great work is to translate our beliefs into action in the way we live our everyday lives.

Ray and Anderson wrote:

Cultural Creatives are redefining what success means, away from success at work and making a lot of money, toward a more soulful life focused on personal fulfilment, social conscience, creating a better future for everyone on the planet.

So the big question we must ask ourselves is: do these ideas, beliefs and values that we claim to hold actually translate into concrete, individual action? Statistics based on attitude surveys and those based on actual consumer behaviour sometimes tell two different stories. It is imperative that we 'walk our talk.'

That inspirational essayist, Wendell Berry, says that the environmental crisis is not really an environmental crisis at all.

It is a people crisis. For it is we, the people, in our day-to-day decisions, who either help to preserve the natural world around us or help to destroy it. When you buy a 'conventional' supermarket banana rather than an organic and Fair Trade one because it seems cheaper, it isn't really. The true cost is the health of an exploited plantation worker you will never meet. Every plastic bag, every litre of petrol, every unnecessary purchase made by every individual has a hidden cost. Those billions of small, everyday decisions are costing the Earth.

So apart from all the other important work we are doing, one of the two most significant contributions we can possibly make is to shift towards a simpler way of life, based on quality, on being, rather than having, getting and spending. It is better for our health, better for our sanity, better for our fellow creatures – human and otherwise – and better for the planet.

Are we doing that? It seems we are starting to. Despite the relentless urging of consumerism, 'downshifting,' as it is called, has been one of the most noticeable social trends of the past decade in the USA and elsewhere, and shows no sign of slowing.

So if you have identified yourself as a Cultural Creative, look around, reach out, keep your heart open, watch for signs. Millions of people share your beliefs, values, hopes and dreams. Together we are creating a new way of life for people on this planet. I call it living green.

But that is not all. Beyond simply living green there is yet another step to take. The other most significant work we do is the work we do on ourselves, on our attitudes, on the way we define who we are. For there is an even more radical way to live. And that is to understand, with your entire mind and body and soul, that you are not simply 'on' the planet, you are an intrinsic part of the planet. You already feel a sense of responsibility for the planet's wellbeing because you really get it that your personal wellbeing and that of the planet are one and the same thing. As above, so below. What is good for the Earth is also good for us. But when you can truly know and feel yourself not as something separate from the Earth, but as a cell in the body of a great living organism we call Gaia, you touch into a deeper level of awareness. And not only to know and understand that but to live your entire life out of that humble knowing, that is deep green living, and that is what this book is about.

– Marian Van Eyk McCain.

*   *   *

PART ONE

PLACE

Let's start by thinking about the human relationship to place.

We all live somewhere. And when we talk about relating more deeply to the Earth that is our greater body, inevitably this leads us to thinking about which particular piece of the Earth we are currently a part of. Along with grass and gulls and rats, we are one of the life forms that has, over millennia, adapted to living in just about any climate. So everywhere you go, there are people living there and having a relationship with the place that gives them sustenance and shelter.

For indigenous people whose tribes and families have lived in one spot for many generations, a knowledge and sense of the region where they live is an extension of their knowledge and sense of self. But for many of us who have grown up in a modern Western culture that places more importance on human-created concepts like nation and city and football team than it does on the ecological divisions of the natural world, that ancient sense of deep identification with one's bioregion has been largely lost. Plus the physical ability to move from area to area has added to the feeling of rootlessness experienced by many. This often forces us to think consciously about place and our relationship to it, which is something no other creature has to do. We get to observe ourselves and how well we fit with our surroundings. We may feel comfortable, we may not. We may know our place well or only slightly or hardly at all. Sometimes we pine for somewhere else. Sometimes we are able to choose to move and to choose a place we think we might prefer. Sometimes work or marriage or other circumstance can land us in a new place we know almost nothing about.

Whatever the situation, the first task of anyone who wants to live a greener life is to get to know, even more fully than they have before, the place to which life has brought them. So we shall start this chapter on place with a very practical list of all the ways in which we can get to know our bioregion. After which we move on to the more subtle aspects of the subject, to what the ancient Romans called the genius loci or what we would now call the 'spirit of place' and we hear some very personal accounts of people's deep immersion in their surroundings and the love and sense of connectedness that arise as a result.

First, then, a very practical list of all the aspects of place.

LEARNING YOUR BIOREGION[1]
Ellen Gunter and Ted Carter

O nce you value something, you never look at it the same way again. It changes you; it becomes a piece of you, however small. And because people today don't know much about where they live, or where their food, water, and energy come from, they don't feel a sense of kinship with it. That, in turn, means that they don't know what's healthy for the section of Earth they occupy. Most of us don't know our area's history, why the streets, rivers, streams, or parks have the names they have. Like mountain ranges and old-growth forests, our neighbourhoods, cities, and counties have histories. The region you live in is steeped in the stories of countless lives lived right under the spot where you eat your meals, read your newspaper, surf the internet, and rest your body. So if you name the components of your neighbourhood, if you grow to love it and feel ownership of it, so that you say—in some form—"this is my tribe," it's not so easy for you to ignore it or let it be strewn with trash, sprayed with pesticides, or poisoned by the runoff from a strip-mining company that's contaminating the ground water.

That's the first part: get to know where you live. Learn what you can about the space that is providing you with oxygen every day of your life. You don't have to love all of it, you don't have to live there forever, but find some little thing to cherish about where you live. It has you in it. You have left pieces of yourself behind every time you exhaled a breath. If we know what is happening in our bioregion that is unhealthy or unsustainable, we can begin to make intelligent decisions about what to do as communities of involved, informed citizens. As resources become more precious and using them wisely and sustainably becomes the new norm, this kind of wisdom is essential. And since so many of us live in cities today, 'urban consciousness' is only going to become more important.

What you are likely to find out is that there are a lot of others in your region who have the same curiosity and concerns. The age of the urban warrior, defending and reinvigorating the health of his or her bioregion has quietly descended upon us. Understanding your bioregion is an important piece in the process of establishing a connection to the earth, because it's the part of the earth where you and people you love spend your lives, where you dream and work and experience the passage of time.

How much do you really know about where you live? See how many of these questions you can answer without looking them up. If you can't answer some questions and decide to find out more, this list will take you a long way toward getting a sense of what's going on in your corner of the earth and how today's news stories – about global warming, oil and gas pipelines, GMOs, and the stability of the earth's food, water, and air resources – may be touching your life. The French philosopher Blaise Pascal said, "The least movement is of importance to all nature. The entire ocean is affected by a pebble." Every effort you make to understand the place you live in opens a door. Inside every door lies the gift of insight.

Water

1. Where does your region get most of its water (reservoir, lake, river, or aquifer)?

2. Has this always been your area's source of water? If not, what other sources has your area drawn from? What condition are those former water sources in now? Get a map of your region and trace the water you drink, from precipitation to tap.

3. How long has it been since the main water lines in your neighbourhood have been replaced? What are they made of (iron,

stainless steel, clay, aluminium, PVC)?

4. Call your local water department to ask what chemicals are in your water.

5. How do you dispose of out-of-date prescriptions and over-the-counter drugs? What disposal practice does your water department recommend? Ask your friends how they get rid of their outdated pharmaceuticals.

6. How does your town rate the quality of your tap water?

7. What is the state of your area's water table? Healthy? High? Low? How long does your water department consider that your present water source will be sufficient for your town's needs?

8. How much rainfall did your area get last year? What about snowfall?

9. When was the last time your area endured a drought?

10. When was the last time a major fire burned in your area?

11. If there is a wildfire season in the bioregion where you live, how many wildfires have you had in the last five years? How many total acres were burned?

Trash

1. Where does your garbage go? How much of the methane coming from your local tip or landfill is being captured and recycled? How can you find out?

2. Where do your recyclables go?

3. In your area, is recycling a law, or is participation voluntary?

4. What are the rules about how it is to be presented for pickup (separated or not, contained in recyclable plastic, boxes broken down and tied, loose/ not loose, and so forth)?

5. What day are recyclables picked up in your neighbourhood?

6. For one week, weigh your trash – both garbage and recyclables. Make a list of ways you can begin to have less to throw out.

Stuff

1. Look at the clothes, shoes, bedding, and towels in your cupboards and drawers. How many come from outside the country? Consider the travel miles involved.

2. Scientist Jane Poynter spent two years living inside Biosphere 2 outside Oracle, Arizona. After breathing clean, unpolluted air for two years, the first thing she noticed when she emerged into the earth's atmosphere in 1993 was, "People stink" – from all the chemicals we put on our bodies and clothes. Identify the substances that you and members of your family use that contain any chemical additives: deodorant, perfume, hair spray and gel, aftershave, mouthwash, fabric softener, room deodorizers, laundry additives and detergents, toilet bowl cleaners, carpet fresheners, and so on.

Energy

1. What is the source for the electrical power and/or heat for your house or apartment?

2. If it's coal, where does your coal come from?

3. If it's nuclear energy – or you live near a nuclear power plant – where does the radioactive waste go? How old is the plant?

4. If it's natural gas, how far does it have to be piped to reach your neighbourhood? How old are the gas lines? Does your gas come from fracked wells in your area? If so, how do they dispose of the fracking wastewater?

5. Do oil pipelines run through your neighbourhood? If so, do they carry tar sands? How old are the pipelines?

6. Is any of your power from solar, wind, or geothermal technology? If so, by what percentage has it grown or declined in the last ten years?

7. Where is the closest wind farm or solar array to where you live? How much of your region's power comes from wind or solar?

8. If you own your home, what would it cost in current prices to

install solar panels and/or a passive solar water heater on your roof?

Who Speaks for You?

1. What are your local school board's plans on the greening of new or existing school buildings? How about civic buildings (police station, court building, firehouse, town hall, and others)?

2. What are the positions of your local and national political representatives on alternative energy? What are their voting records? How much money have fossil fuel, nuclear, or 'big ag' interests contributed to their campaigns?

Your Little Corner of the World: Your Neighborhood

1. With two days' leeway, how many days has it been since the last full moon – or when is the next full moon?

2. Based on the various soil types, what soil series (sand, clay, and so on) is your home built on?

3. What is the industrial history of your area?

4. Name five native regional plants and the months that make up their growing season.

5. From what direction do winter storms generally come in your region? Include all storm types that apply

6. On the longest day of the year, when does the sun set where you live? What about the shortest day of the year?

7. Name five of the grasses that grow in your area. Are any of them native?

8. What spring wildflower is consistently among the first to bloom where you live?

9. Name five resident and five migratory birds in your area. When do they nest and produce young?

10. What primary ecological event or process determined the landform of your town or city?

11. What species have become extinct in your area?

12. From where you're reading this, point north.

13. What direction does your head point when you sleep?

14. Point to where the sun rises on your residence.

15. How many people live in your rural parish, town or city? In general, is the population increasing or decreasing?

16. What is the air quality in your area, on average? How many days last year were environmental alerts issued?

17. What are the local or county regulations regarding the use of pesticides in parks and public areas? In gardens? On farms? Golf courses? Are any warnings required for their use?

18. Do highway departments in your city and county use chemical pesticides and/ or fertilizers on the green areas (medians, exits, greenspaces) along public highways and roads? If so, what kind? What do you know about their long-term effects on humans, animals, birds, insects, and the soil? (Hint: Google them.)

Food

1. What are the main agricultural products of your region?

2. How long is your region's agricultural growing season?

3. If applicable, when are arable crops harvested in the summer?

4. Is GMO labelling mandatory where you live?

5. Where are the closest farmers' markets in your area? When are they open?

6. Do you belong to a CSA or food co-op? Do you know how to find one in your neighbourhood or town?

7. Do you know how to plant and tend to a vegetable or herb garden? How to grow one without chemical pesticides or fertilizers?

8. Do you know how to start and maintain an organic compost heap?

9. Can you name at least two farmers who raise organic meat or grow organic vegetables or fruit near you?

10. Do you know how to shop for fresh, chemical-free produce?

11. Where did your last purchase of fresh fruit come from? How about the ingredients for your next salad? The last vegetables you served? If your produce came from other countries, what do you know about their food safety laws?

12. A 'locavore' is someone who eats food that comes from within about one hundred miles of home. Become more aware of how you nourish yourself Begin by taking stock. Examine the contents of your cupboard, refrigerator, and freezer. Note how many items come from more than one hundred miles away.

13. Do your local schools serve healthy lunches? How much that food is fresh and local? Organic?

* * *

Editor's Note:

1. This article has been adapted from the authors' book *Earth Calling: A Climate Change Handbook for the 21st Century*, North Atlantic Books, 2014, pp: 232-238. There is a review of *Earth Calling* on our book review website – see: http://greenspirit.org.uk/bookreviews/2014/08/earth-calling-a-climate-change-handbook-for-the-21st-century-by-ellen-gunter-and-ted-carter/

LEARNING TO LOVE PLACE THROUGH DWELLING

Donna Ladkin

I have this idea which won't let go of me. I have this idea that at least part of the current ecological situation in which we find ourselves has its roots in our lost capacity to relate to place. Not just 'relate' to place, but LOVE place. And most importantly, to LOVE the place we find ourselves in, right here, right now. The global ecological crisis is just too big for me to get hold of. Every time I think of it I feel overwhelmed, small, impotent. Any change I make seems insignificant when juxtaposed against the actions of governments and corporations which seem oblivious, if not downright in contempt of, the impact of their policies on the planet.

The very infra-structure which supports my materially comfortable way of life as a citizen of the UK is itself in many ways in opposition to a more ecologically sensitive way of relating to place. But, I have another little seedling of a notion, that loving place actually could play some part in promoting the kinds of changes on the kind of scale which could make a difference.

I wonder what would happen if we learned to love place, this place, the one that we are living in right now? Would that love provide the emotional impetus we need to be more mindful and choiceful about how we live in that place? Others seem to be writing about 'love of place' and the possibilities it engenders in different ways. David Orr writes about ecoliteracy. Sawyer writes about bioregionalism. Freya Matthews writes about 'nativism' Stephanie Mills writes about 're-inhabitation'. Certainly, indigenous peoples seem to engage with the Earth in ways informed by a deep knowing, respect for, and love of the place in which they live. The tack I'm keen to pursue is that environmentalism (or ethical relationship with place, my preferred handle on this) is not just about saving the Amazon forest (although that is important). It is not about saving endangered species (although that is important, too). It is about growing into a right relationship with wherever a person is, right here and right now. Fundamentally, I am suggesting, such a relationship can be fostered through 'dwelling'. This essay charts the beginnings of my own journey in learning to love and understand the significance of place in my own life. I hope it may act as an impetus for you to think about your relationship with the places you inhabit, and to grow into 'right relation' to that place, right here and right now.

Beginnings

The following words offered by the Native American educator, Gregory Cajete, remain an important touchstone for me. He writes: "As you begin your journey to find this ancient indigenous mind-set, think about who you are and who you represent. Understand that each of us, in our own small way is a vital link within the context of creating an educational process that allows for a sustainable way of living. Whether this role you play is large or small, know that it has an effect... And as you move from that mountain down the pathway to begin a renewed journey of ecological thought and action, think about the journey of our life in relationship to 'place'. Keep in view the fact that your journey can be a very important part of the transformation of education that must take place in this next generation."[1]

What is the State of Dwelling in our Precarious Age?

I do not know the source of the water which flows from my tap when I turn the faucet on. I do not know the mechanism by which the water becomes hot. I do not know the source of the fuel which causes the water to be hot. I do not know where the water goes when it runs down the drain at the front of my kitchen. I watch the rising and falling of the river behind the house. It bears no relation to the pressure of the water flowing from my kitchen tap. And I am too busy to find out. How would I find out? Who would I ask? I am busy, writing my paper about dwelling practices. I am busy cutting vegetables (the source of which I do not know) cooking them on my cooker (what coal is being burnt where, to heat up my carrots?) The one thing I do know is that the carrot tops which I have cut, tomorrow morning I will bring to the compost heap at the bottom of the steps leading to the garden. And there, they will combine with the leaves which have fallen from the oak trees, and the other vegetable scraps I deposited yesterday, and the rain, and the bird droppings. And, through mysterious processes, (which probably involve Heidegger's Divinities) they will be transformed into dark, friable earth. Which will be spread on the grounds here at the Castle and grow the rhododendrons, and the buddleia and more oak trees. Which will give off oxygen. Which I will breathe. Is this the beginning of dwelling?

The two phrases which keep coming back to me are: 'Think of who you are and what you represent,' and, 'think about the journey of your life in relation to place'. I offer you my response to these questions. Who I am And What I Represent. I am a 45-year old American woman of mixed racial background – my father is African American and Native American and my mother is of German and French Canadian heritage. I've chosen to live in England for half of my life, now, and England very much feels like 'home' now. When people ask why I stay, I say, "Because of the footpaths!" I think of Maine as my American home, and that is where I say I am 'from' when people ask, even though I was born in Washington DC and lived in Maryland for the first ten years of my life.

The move from Maryland to Maine instigated a total change in the way my family lived. For instance, instead of driving from place to place, walking and cycling became our main mode of transport (or skiing, in the winter!) We bought a house in the tiny village of Caribou (population 10,000 and falling), nestled on the banks of the Aroostook River, fourteen miles south of the Canadian border. Northern Maine is not the picture- postcard coastal region normally associated with the state. It is a land of gentle hills put to agricultural use, pristine lakes, and trees. The Allagash wilderness, which comprises two-thirds of Aroostook County's landspace, still contains some of the only virgin timber found anywhere on the North American continent.[2]

When we moved to Caribou, we were living in the vicinity of wild places. And we responded by running wild. Because of my mother's working patterns, the three of us 'Lucas kids' were largely left to our own devices outside school hours. During the winter months (November to May) we ice skated every evening, built snow tunnels and caves, and skied (but this was not the skiing of resorts and chair-lifts, it was the skiing of strap some skies to your feet, find a hill and let rip!). Summers were spent picking wild berries which grew in the field behind our house, swimming in the nearby lakes, cycling, roaming through woods, learning to live outside.

We were poor, monetarily (as were most of the folk who live in Aroostook County). But I don't remember feeling poor. I spent hours sitting in my favourite tree reading book after book borrowed from the mobile library which stopped right outside of our house, a luxury which my currently well-off life seldom provides me.

Life revolved around the weather and changing seasons in Caribou. At that time, the livelihood of the community depended on the harvesting of the potato crop. Harvesting potatoes was a community endeavour. Schools started in mid-August in order that they could close again for three weeks in September and October when school children would take to the fields to bring in the crop.

Everyone was involved in this activity, children picked, teachers drove trucks that collected the 150 lb barrels of potatoes, shop owners kept their shops open later hours so that food could be purchased once the sun set.

When I left Aroostook county I remember reading sociology articles about the North of Maine being one of the most poverty stricken areas of the US. I remember the horrified tones in which one article cited the fact that it was a place where children as young as seven or eight were forced to pick potatoes each autumn. Horrors! In my view, it was always the few rich kids whose parents didn't allow them out into the fields who missed out.

I don't want to overromanticise the situation either. Four out of the nine children in my mother's family have MS (including my mother) and I often wonder if there is any connection between the development of the disease in them and chemicals (including DDT) which were used to kill the potato tops. During every harvest season there were inevitable accidents, kids were crushed by barrels or trucks, hands were caught in machinery, fingers lost. The point of telling this story is to notice what it was about this time which helped foster my capacity to relate to place. For certainly, I believe living in Caribou enabled me to develop a strong sensitivity and connection to that place, as well as a way of relating to subsequent places in which I've lived.

Thinking back, there are three aspects of that experience which seem particularly important. Firstly, there was a sense of 'pace' which was important. This operated on two levels, attention to a 'here and now' pace, and awareness of the larger natural cycles of death and re-birth in which the here and now is embedded. Life in Caribou often seemed imbued with a sense of endless hours, unpressured time in which to explore and BE in the places we chose to inhabit (be they trees, fields, or even my bedroom). In my ongoing inquiry into dwelling a recurrent theme both practically and theoretically, is the importance of pace and rhythm for engaging with human as well as nonhuman worlds. 'Slowing down' (for in our times of frenetic activity it is more often slowing down than speeding up which is needed!) is a key practice any one of us interested in engaging more meaningfully with place can try, right here, right now!

The second key aspect in developing my connection with Caribou relates closely to pace, but brings with it a different quality – the quality associated with 'play'. Perhaps one of the reasons so often when I speak with people about the significance of 'place' in their lives they recount stories from their childhood is because childhood is the time in which 'play' is a legitimate part of what we do. And playing in place seems crucial in developing a relationship with place. Playing fosters openness, curiosity, reciprocity; all important elements of 'dwelling' and developing the awareness of how place impacts on us, just as we impact on it.

Finally, dwelling in Caribou was a project enacted by the entire community. Together, we charted the rainfall that nourished the potato crop, together we celebrated the first blossom with the crowning of the 'Potato Blossom Queen', together we got muddy and tired and sore from the back-breaking work of bringing in each autumn's harvest. Such community rituals provided a powerful means by which we jointly acknowledged and remembered the source of our sustenance – the very place we lived. I'm sure there are other aspects of my personal history which could account for my desire to learn to relate to place in a loving way. However, these three; pace, play and community, stand out as having been particularly relevant. Moreover, I'm suggesting they could be embodied in practices such as: Paying attention to our pace so that we notice the place we inhabit. Making time for play and exploration. Building communities to celebrate together the rhythms and cycles of our particular locality which might further foster our love for, and desire to care for the place in which we live, right here, and right now.

* * *

Notes

1. Cajete, Gregory. *Indigenous Education and Ecology* in John Grim (Ed), *Indigenous Traditions and Ecology*, Harvard University Press, 2001, pp. 619-638.
2. This is particularly significant when you realise that Aroostook County is the size of Wales.

Donna Ladkin is Professor of Leadership and Ethics at Plymouth Graduate School of Management, Plymouth University. Her background in music and philosophy informs much of her work in the areas of leadership and aesthetics, and aesthetic approaches to business ethics. She is the author of a number of books including *Mastering the Ethical Dimension of Organizations*, which uses art based methods in a reflective approach to developing ethical astuteness. Home is Devon where she lives with her husband and flat-coated retriever Zelda, with whom she explores the local lanes, Dartmoor and coastal walks as part of her daily dwelling practice. This essay was first published in the GreenSpirit Journal in Winter 2005.

SHEEP AND ART:
AN EXPERIMENT IN
CONNECTED LIVING
Helen Cockburn

I am writing this on a hot May afternoon. Insects of various descriptions are crawling on my arms and legs and scuttling across the pages of my notebook. The hawthorn hedges which surround me are a mass of fragrant white blossom; oak and ash trees are in full leaf; dandelions stand proud of fading cowslips and a waving crowd of puffballs jostles between buttercups, cow parsley and groundsel. A blue tit preens himself on the branch of an ash tree as a pair of swallows swoop and soar in the cornflower blue sky. This is Greenhaven, our home in northeast Suffolk where for the past two years we have been building an organic smallholding with ecology and creativity at its heart.

Our journey here began with a growing awareness that we needed to make changes in our lives. It's becoming a very familiar story. My husband was becoming increasingly dissatisfied with corporate life – especially after a round of redundancies during which he represented the interests of those employees considered surplus to requirements. In trying to negotiate these redundancies with dignity and fairness he found his personal values stretched to breaking point. We were also becoming more and more disillusioned with a monoculture which measures everything on an increasingly dubious scale of economic values and incredulous at the constant striving for economic growth regardless of the fact that the 'success' it signifies only magnifies the very inequalities and dissatisfactions it purports to dispel. A system which, as the playwright Edward Bond put it, "creates inequality with contrived wants".

Wendell Berry has written of this separation of people, places and products from their histories as being one of the primary needs of industrialism; a process of detachment which means that UK supermarkets now sell 80% of all the food we eat at home, supermarket delivery lorries account for 40% of lorry traffic on our roads, and we spend three times more on ready meals than any other country in Europe.

Another feature of this dislocation has been the reduction of sentient beings to mere commodities in a system of industrialised agriculture (surely an oxymoron?) which means that it is almost impossible for us otherwise unrepentant carnivores to square our consciences with current farming practice. So, refusing any longer to be identified solely as 'consumers' and lamenting this increasing disconnection between ourselves and the Earth we decided to stop being armchair critics and try to create an alternative – following Gandhi's philosophy of being the change you want to see.

We spent a year trying to decide what exactly this would mean: slowly building a vision of where we wanted to be; researching what was possible; devouring an entire library of books; visiting the Centre for Alternative Technology at Machynlleth, Wales, compiling endless lists... We wanted some land, certainly. But how much? And what could we afford? Staying where we were was out of the question – north Hertfordshire is a beautiful but expensive part of the country. We had gravitated east towards the Suffolk coast for several years, seduced by its haunted coastline of crumbling sand and glittering sea, sweeping skies and endless horizons, so making the decision to move here was easy. Eventually we were able to make a straight swap between our village house with its small back garden and Greenhaven, a three hundred year-old former blacksmith's and wheelwright's.

The house needed renovating but had the irresistible advantage of ten acres which had been organically cultivated for almost thirty years. By the time we moved in my husband had completed a part-time agricultural course and resigned from his job, retraining as a coach and therapist. Our aim at Greenhaven is to create a connected living and working environment in which the senses and imagination are stimulated.

The idea of the genius loci or spirit of place is very close to our hearts; an awareness of the powerful energies contained in every landscape, most commonly symbolised by the archetype of the Green Man. For us, the expression of this creative spirit is an essential part of forming a meaningful relationship with any locality. We feel a deep sense of stewardship for these ten acres, aware that whatever we do here will become an indelible part of its history, for better or worse. In a practical sense we have found that concentrated observation of our everyday environment has been our best teacher. This simple act of paying attention and taking notice of the minutiae of where we live, comparing it day by day and season by season, has helped us become a great deal more aware of our surroundings and our impact on them.

For example, our apple orchard contains nineteen varieties, including Lord Lambourne, Easter Orange, Norfolk Royal (still laden with crimson apples in the snow of late February), Newton Wonder, Egremont Russet, Merton Knave and our personal favourite, Ashmead Kernel. Each fruit is uniquely different in size, shape, colour, taste, smell and texture. We were keen not to take for granted our first abundant harvest (which produced excellent juice and cider) so we duly Wassailed the orchard with friends one cold, wet evening last January as a sign of our gratitude, hoping for an equally good crop this year. We splashed the tree roots with cider before consuming a glass or two of the heady concoction ourselves then crammed leftover Christmas cake into the heart of the bough.

Traditionally this should have been followed by firing a shotgun over the branches but we agreed to substitute party poppers in order to prevent the premature demise of our Southdown sheep who were grazing innocently in an adjoining field.

In our first year we have grown potatoes, tomatoes, courgettes, cucumbers, peppers and aubergines and planted almost thirty trees – hawthorn, elder, birch, hazel, damson, dogwood, birch and mulberry. We have cleared and burnt debris from the massive old ditch (or moat, which once marked the boundary between farm and common land). Three new fields have been fenced and hedged with blackthorn, whitethorn and hawthorn, along with ash and oak saplings to plug gaps and protect us from the bitterly cold north-easterlies. One day we hope to have a polytunnel here and perhaps a small wind turbine. A large open field skirts our northern boundary, an everyday reminder of the kind of farming we don't want to echo here – oversprayed, overcultivated and oversized

By privileging science as our sole means of knowing, rather than as one method among many, we have neglected the imagination to such an extent that art is often regarded as just another commodity and reported almost exclusively in this context (the record price paid for a painting by Picasso and the destruction of Charles Saatchi's collection in a warehouse fire are just two recent examples). Art as a soulful activity, as a vital connector between mind and matter, is virtually ignored. Emily Dickinson said that Nature is "a haunted house, but art a house that wants to be haunted" yet as we continue to dismantle the house of Nature it is hardly surprising that the house of art has lost some of its magical atmosphere. But the phenomenal success of 'Sun', Olafur Eliasson's beautiful installation at Tate Modern, shows that there is a widespread hunger for art concerned with such meaning (despite the fact that the Tate's commentary makes it clear that any spiritual associations are to be regarded as incompatible with the work's 'exposed structure', as if by understanding the 'how' of something we necessarily negate the mystery of 'what').

At Greenhaven we plan to build into our landscape elements of contemplative stillness and surprise, including walking a maze of herbs along spiralling footpaths so that the air is filled with the scent of rosemary, thyme and oregano; sculptures and totems; assemblages of natural objects; trees dressed with fluttering ribbons carrying messages into the air, and, more conventionally, a small gallery attached to our framing workshop and studio.

A great inspiration for us has been Kettle's Yard in Cambridge, once the home of Jim Ede, a curator at the Tate Gallery, and his wife Helen. They filled their house with modern art while retaining all the qualities of a domestic space. Ede spoke of people being prevented from seeing art because of what he called the 'functional eye'; a way of seeing which insists on seeing 'correctly'. This is fine for judging the distance between, say, a teacup and a sugar bowl, for making adjustments in distance and direction but, as Ede so rightly said, 'in the arts none of this matters'. Art instead enables us to constantly re-imagine possibilities; it engages us with questions of meaning in energised form. But as 'doing' (producing, building, profiting) has become synonymous with living, 'being' (imagining, enjoying, connecting) has come to be identified with that most terrible of modern sins, inefficiency, and the reflection which is an integral part of the imaginative process interpreted as idleness. There seem fewer and fewer accessible secret places, both interior and exterior.

The kind of aimless wandering conducive to the imagination always takes place on the margins, in those liminal spaces where one thing shifts into something else, however briefly: dawn, dusk, the slow passage of one season into another, a walk along a field margin or through an orchard path flanked by hawthorn and apple blossom. At Greenhaven sheep and art co-exist as symbols of the earthy soul and the skyward spirit, with ourselves hovering at the intersection, weaving a way between the spirit as it soars and the soul as it descends, tethering each to the other, reconciling and balancing both, while remaining aware of their complementary yet distinctive natures. As John Updike said, it is the duty of art "to give the mundane its beautiful due".

The Green family lived here in the house which still bears their name for more than three hundred years. The last of them, Corporal Oakley Scott Green, scratched his name into the soft red brick beside the front window and was killed in France in October 1918. His father and grandfather bore the same name and a carved oak tree sprouting giant acorns adorns the fireplace in our sitting room. Alongside our twelve Southdowns we now have thirty chickens, a refurbished workshop which houses our framing business and gallery, a renovated wheelwright's shop soon to provide self-contained holiday accommodation, a coaching and therapy practice, and last but not least a house which has become a home. In a financial sense this project will be a risk for the foreseeable future – but in every other way we are immeasurably richer than before. We believe passionately in what we are doing here and our aim is to establish a not-for-profit trust so that we can share our experiences with others and provide a resource for exploring the ideas sketched out here. Creating Greenhaven is a process, an ongoing experiment in connected living and as such we have no sense of either 'success' or 'failure'. It is simply our way of weaving depth and meaning into life and will continue in some form or another for as long as we can make that happen. Slowly, quietly, the genius loci of Greenhaven is re-emerging.

*   *   *

Helen Cockburn is an artist and writer. This essay was first published in the GreenSpirit Journal in Summer 2004.

GREEN AND BELONGING

Marianne Worley

The Gift

I was eight years old when my father told me a terrible secret about green. "Did you know," he said as we stood in the garden one summer morning, "that plants are everything but green? They send out light at a wavelength that we call green, so it is really the only colour that plants are not".

Trying to think about this was like grasping out in slow motion for the tail of a fleeing tiger. I had to keep grasping and chasing until in a flash, for a moment, I had it – the sky was everything but blue, the earth of this island continent anything but red, and I was every colour except pale pink. Perhaps he could hear the rumble of shifting foundations. "Maybe you could think of it like a present, a gift. The greenness of plants is what they give to you – like the carbon dioxide that you breathe out and they breathe in, and the trick is to hold their green within you."

Beginning

My father was an engineer, a rock-climber, a walker. His gaze, by natural inclination, was directed outwards and upwards, towards the horizon and the sky. My mother watched smaller things – a ripple, a feather. Her childhood world was the grime and glitter of Mexico City punctuated by longed-for trips to the sea; my father's was the hedgerow-lined roads of an English village, and the fields where he collected bird eggs and threw conkers.

I was 22 months old when my parents arrived in Australia and my favourite memories of growing up here are of exploring. My brother and I, let loose to beach-comb while our parents set up camp, found shark egg cases and stranded jellies, built driftwood tepees. Once we spent the week trying to light a fire using two pieces of flint and another time we ground up handfuls and handfuls of wattle seed to make damper and ended up with only enough flour to fill a thimble.

Somewhere along the limestone coast of South Australia, a ranger taught us how to find wild fruits in the bush. At my first taste of the salty, white berries of the coastal bearded-heath I resolved to become a ranger – a real one, one who strides the land and fends for herself, sword at the ready. Tolkien's trilogy, which I happened to be reading at the time, undeniably helped fuel these dreams, no matter that there were no female rangers in Middle Earth. While I waited to become old enough to walk the wilds alone, there were David Attenborough documentaries on Sundays to be feasted on, the black belly of the night sky to lie beneath, and always, the ocean to be scanned for any sign of whale or mermaid.

Finding Home
The landscape that we walked, canoed and camped in, was the backdrop for my early dreaming. I saw fairies in the fern-gullies, trolls under bridges, the sprites and secret things of a folklore transported from Europe, all the while being only vaguely aware that this landscape whispered an even older mythology.

My awakening to this deeper land began when my parents suggested that the pine trees in the dark, lifeless plantations and the willows that choked the creek near our house had left some of their spirit behind in their old countries. I pondered this as I climbed to the top of the liquidambar tree in our front yard. I had tried to rouse this tree; I had sung to it and confided in it; yet it was true, ours had always been a one-way friendship. From this point on, I began to befriend eucalypts. They always hummed with life; moths and lorikeets visited their flowering branches, caterpillars and leaf-suckers pillaged their leaves. These trees knew no other home. Shaped by millennia, they knew to hold their leaves at an angle to the relentless southern sun, how to suck the barest of nutrients from ancient soil and how to resurrect their lives after fire.

Where was my home? With a family whose lineage was spread across the globe, my sense of displacement was inevitably encouraged. My separation from all those who were considered 'Australian' was reflected in my passport, in my birth certificate. It wasn't until I was sixteen that I realized that my mother had written my name on her citizenship certificate in addition to her own. So I really was an Australian citizen. What that actually meant to me at the time was harder to define.

Australia is a country walked by first, second, third generation immigrants, people uncertain of their right to tread this land and many who live their lives never speaking with an indigenous Australian. We are a people mostly closeted in suburbia, in lives studded with shopping centres and spanned by the fastest road from our house to the city. Yet, the deep history of this country is not in its architecture, in its cathedrals or pubs, it is not in the steel camps that we call our cities; it is in the topsoil that has blown off our farmlands, in the deep water that has risen to the surface to salt the earth. The history of Australia is the history of the land.

Crossing the River

My father died of cancer when I was eighteen. We lived near our choice of city cemeteries but decided to bury him in a bush cemetery amongst the hills that overlook Melbourne. We used an un-sculpted rock for his headstone and planted native wildflowers on his grave from the places that he had loved to walk. Wandering amongst the tombstones, I read the inscriptions. There are other people here who knew, with intimacy, the curve of a special mountain range or the seasonal patterns of a beloved patch of bushland; who having known and loved this land so well, were loathe to leave it. This bush graveyard is the sort of place that my father might have chosen for himself, a place with eucalypts and parrots, where orchids and sundews grow in the cracked clay and skinks bask on the basalt rocks that line his grave.

On our bushwalks he would always hold out his hand at the faster-flowing rivers, guide my feet carefully onto each rock. It was this way that I came here, to this side of the water.

Listening to the Landscape

I am driving out again, up into the mountain catchment area of Melbourne's water supply, to a world that is hidden to most of us who drink the clear water that finally reaches the city of Melbourne. I'll stand at the beginning of the tiny, muddy trickles where the great rivers that feed our dams are born. Up here, in the small remnants of cool temperate rainforest that once dominated Gondwanaland, I will sit for hours, taking in the secrets of green.

These small fragments of forest are but a shadow of what they once were, a memory of a time before Australia became a child of fire. Mountain Ash, Eucalyptus regnans, the tallest hardwood and flowering plant on earth, encroaches on the rainforest from all sides. It is a master of fire. Its bark drips like oil-soaked rags, its limbs crack and fall about it to create a pyre for a king waiting to die in a blaze so that a new generation can emerge from a nutrient-rich bed of ash.

The rainforest that once reigned here has been pushed further and further into the coolest, deepest gullies and has taken its diverse plant and animal life along with it. Myrtle Beech and Southern Sassafras are the two main tree species that make up this forest. Unlike the tropical rainforests of the world, the diversity here is not to be found in these higher plants, but at the smaller scale – in the mosses and liverworts, the fungi, lichens and the countless invertebrates. The mosses are forests of their own to a world of minutiae; to nematodes, mites and trillions of other microscopic life-forms. Little aliens on little planets of their own.

Mountain Ash eucalypts, a hundred metres high, line the rainforest edge. These trees have escaped the tongues of fire that periodically lap the rainforest boundary and hence grow to be the oldest of the giants. Those that are over a hundred years old begin to develop hollows in their trunks and limbs that become homes for owls, parrots, bats and creatures like the Leadbeater's Possum, a tiny, nocturnal marsupial that lives amongst these giant trees and which was believed to be extinct for half a century before it was rediscovered in the early 1960s. Some people call it the 'fairy possum' because it moves like a silent, fleeting shadow and is shy of a spotlight beam. Late at night in these tall forests, you can sometimes hear the gurgling-shriek of the Yellow-bellied Glider, a tree-dwelling marsupial with a membrane of skin between its front and hind legs that allows it to glide between trees. These animals are the acrobats of the canopy and will hide behind a tree trunk if you shine a spotlight at them. Others, like the Greater Glider, sit still in a spotlight beam, their moon-yellow eyes round and reflective in the dark.

In contrast to the eucalypt forest, only a few mammals enter the deep, moss-laden rainforest where I carry out my fieldwork. One of these is a mouse-sized marsupial, the Antechinus, a voracious insectivore and Australia's answer to lions, tigers and bears. I take a warped delight in telling people the bizarre life story of this animal: all the male Antechinuses live for less than a year and then die in an exhausted frenzy of mating, leaving the pregnant females to rear their young alone. You can occasionally see Antechinuses scurrying around the base of Myrtle Beech trees near dusk. By day I come across black, beetle carapaces, remnants of their nightly feasts. Other, larger creatures dwelt here once. Sometimes a moving shadow behind a tree fern will trick me into thinking I've just seen a fast-running dinosaur ducking for cover.

I crush up a Sassafras leaf and the scent of nutmeg spiced with citrus assails me. If you come across the root of a Sassafras while crawling amidst ferns and across soft orange carpets of Myrtle Beech leaves, you've no need to look up to know what tree species this root belongs to; the beguiling fragrance leaks out of the very pores of the wood. Every sense is aroused when wandering around this place. Kneeling on the stem of a fallen tree fern, I'm assaulted with the pungent odour of a crushed liverwort – 'like the stale oil smell of an old garage' is how this species is described in one reference book. Another two liverwort species that hang in dark green veils from the trunks of the Sassafras can only be distinguished by sniffing their crushed cells. It is a gamble that you take every time – one smells like sweet, moist earth mixed with the scent of parsnips, while the other exudes the stench of mothballs.

In damp areas along the river edge, umbrella mosses stand up and away from the wet ground like miniature tree ferns. In cavernous hollows created by the root systems of the Myrtle Beech, mosses glow like fireflies in the weak rays of the slanting sun. While poking around the tree roots scoring moss abundance, scrub-wrens follow me; the long hours I spend in the same spot gives them enough time to recognize that this ungainly animal poses no threat. They take advantage of the insects that I stir up in the leaf litter with each step.

Down in the gully, a male lyrebird calls. He scrapes away the leaf litter from a round patch of earth to create a stage upon which to dance and practise his courtship songs that mimic every bird in the forest with uncanny accuracy. What gives him away is that he makes each call as loud as the last, whether he is imitating the far-flinging cry of a whip-bird or the soft chattering of a wren.

Take a ten-minute stroll along a path through these forests and you might come across a lyrebird, but you'd see it for only a few seconds before it shrieks and wings off down-slope, back into the forest depths. If you are quiet enough, you might sneak up on one and watch it scraping the earth in search of grubs with its huge chicken-like feet.

To study moss diversity in the rainforest, I spend two hours at a time crawling around a single eight by eight metre plot. It is at these times that I have had the best encounters with lyrebirds. They hear me making noise; sometimes humming to myself as I work. Even if I am silent, they are soon aware of my presence, and after some time, curiosity overcomes their wariness. Once, a lyrebird walked right up and stared at me for several minutes. Perhaps it wondered what sort of creature I was, or it imagined that I had found a particularly good patch for foraging. Maybe it thought I needed more practice with my courtship songs. I don't know what went through the mind of that lyrebird in those poised moments when we peacefully surveyed each other; all I know is how rare this encounter was for me, a human, in front of whose noise and haste all other creatures usually flee.

I am an earth astronaut on a space-walk when I enter the forest – my lifeline, like Hansel and Gretel's breadcrumbs, pieces of fluorescent pink flagging-tape tied up at intervals behind me as I walk. I often wonder whether I'm the only human to have stepped here or there, but I know that this is an illusion. These ancient forests shrink from fire and are a relic of a time long since passed, a time before people. Yet, for at least 60,000 years, the Australian landscape has been walked by humans. This landscape has been managed by fire, by people from the oldest of earth's living cultures.

The Wurundjeri people, whose country is the southern section of this mountain range as well as its valleys and plains, have certainly known these rainforests. Their ancestors came to gather stems of the Austral Mulberry for fire-sticks and no doubt to collect the cool, clear water from the streams that flow down now, through pipes, into our homes. They know that when the lyrebird is courting, calling its song, that the season, one of seven here, not four, is changing once again. These people then, with such deep knowing, must have entered under the Myrtle Beeches for the beauty and spirit of this place alone. I do not know if they ever called the rainforest home. It is too cold, too wet, and harbours too few mammals or edible plants; certainly it is no place to hunt or to sleep.

I know that it is not my home. My grandparents never told me stories about this land. I am a naked, white baby in these forests. Yet somehow, this ancient place seems to have always been present in the hidden depths of the human psyche. Anyone who walks beneath the gnarled and knotted boughs of a Myrtle Beech will feel instant recognition. It is a story place, a fairy tale place. And perhaps it is one of those few places that can never be a true home for a human. Wildness still lingers here. Otherworldliness.

Sometimes I sit in the forest, knowing that everything is reaching, growing and dying around me. It amazes me that I can't tell, that I can't hear limbs stretching and see leaves unfolding – that it all just seems so still.

To be able to experience such things, to see, hear, smell and touch such things, to step outside the normal scale of human life, is a great privilege. Even if it is only in the moments that your nose is up close to the bark of a tree and you can see its rivulets and canyons like lines in an ancient face, or if it is to look through a microscope or a telescope to see how the universe extends either side of you into infinity.

My father once suggested to me that there is no ultimate why question; that in the end there is only how and what. I grappled with this for a long time. Surely, the why questions, why things are the way they are, why we are here, are the deepest we can ask. After a time though, these sorts of questions seemed to lose their meaning. Do we demand a reason for the life of every rock and tree? Is it really so terrifying that there may be no ultimate purpose? Perhaps it is only our human mind that requires this logic of fundamental cause and effect. I don't know, but somehow, being away from the cities, on some rocky outcrop or in a forested gully, the why begins to melt away, and what becomes more and more beautiful and soul-quenching to me is simply … being.

On occasion, someone or other has suggested that spending time in the natural world is escaping from the real world. To this I assert that the lives of other creatures are as real as our own. Rocks and rivers, the deep sea and the space between the planets, these are all as real as a bank note, more real in fact. There is beauty in the truth that surrounds me here. This beauty is not an abstraction or a distraction from reality. The dark, decaying fungus, the spider that blends into the lichen, the snail, the leech, these are also true. Truth is beautiful and ugly all at once, and it is neither of these things alone; nor is it good or evil. I forget what these words mean and I'm left wanting only to embrace it all, to acknowledge that I am, we are, also part of this. All I know is that in these moments, when the leech does not bite and the rain does not seep into my clothing, I sit with it all, in the sunlight, in peace, and delight in simply being. There is no conflict here between beautiful escapism and mundane reality. It is all real, all shiveringly wonderful.

I love the solitude of my fieldwork; I get less and less lonely by the day and become more and more connected with those things and people that I truly care about. Our engagement with the world outside our doorstep, our empathy with other living things, I feel begins with this connection with the natural world. Perhaps if, like many cultures of old, each person was to spend some time alone in a wild place, if we were all given the space and solitude to seek secrets on our own, we might begin to believe in the courage and compassion that we have within ourselves. I wonder if we all could do with a little less loneliness and a little more solitude.

If my soul were to have a home, and the restless spirit of my travelling forebears could be eased, then this forest is where it would be. Some days, it's true, I long for the sky, for rocks and dry places, such is the dampness of my mossy dwelling place. And I miss the stars, the Southern Cross to guide me. But how is this so very different from living in the city with a dark roof over my head and too much light to drown out the stars?

I don't think that most of the inhabitants of the rainforest notice me as I come and go at hasty animal pace. For these ancient things, I exist between the long ticks of a clock, the way moss grows in the fissures between tree roots or in the gaps between paving stones.

City

I pack my car, ready to return to the city, filled with optimism, my senses fully engaged and seeking to integrate the world of humans with the world of other beings. As I approach the city of Melbourne, I see that this integration will be a difficult task.

It begins with the drive back home. As I wind down the mountain roads, the trees lean in and I soar on their grace. I notice the way the sun shines through them and how many colours go to make up that eucalypt green. As I drive away from the deep mountain soils, the trees gradually lose their grand stature. They begin to thin and dry. Houses appear, cars begin to surround me, traffic lights shine red and bright. Trees are replaced by shops and billboards and I read each advertisement as avidly I read the landscape only minutes before; my filtering mechanism yet to be engaged.

The advertising increases, shop names, street signs begin to bombard me; I'm still trying to read them all, notice it all, take it all in. By the time I near my inner city street my stress levels have risen and my mind has become filled with things that I didn't want to know. The noise is constant now, traffic, trams, trains, construction work. The green has faded to grey and I am exhausted. I can't do it, it doesn't make sense to keep all my senses engaged now. I switch off and I am sad.

Sad that I can't breathe in a lungful of clean air, disappointed later on, that I don't notice much as I walk down the street to buy some milk. I begin to feel a greater loneliness, surrounded by the swell of humanity, than in the so-called isolation of the bush. I feel suspended in the city air, ungrounded, disconnected. I close off, reduce my stride length, deflate and stare down at the pavement.

A Green Space

In this state I have forgotten the last small, yet poignant entity that was released from Pandora's box. I begin to feel it stirring within; its bird-like fluttering insistent, even against the strident effusions of the city.

It tells me that I carry something of that forest place within me now and that something of me will always be left there. Green gets into you this way, through all the cracks, all the spaces in between. And now I see it, tucked into a crack between the slabs of concrete beneath my feet, hope dressed in green – a silver-tipped moss – welcoming me home.

* * *

Marianne Worley was born in the UK and grew up in Australia. After a year of wandering the world, she now lives in Healesville, Australia, with her partner and two young children. She is a trained biologist with an honours degree in botany and zoology and a Ph.D. in rainforest bryophyte ecology. She has been involved in a variety of research and biodiversity conservation projects, including threatened species conservation for the Victorian government, radio-tracking koalas, possums and platypus, and contributing authorship of Lonely Planet Publications' *Watching Wildlife – Australia*.

PART TWO

LIFESTYLES

From thinking about where we live, we now move on to the subject of how we live. If we live simply, it is perfectly possible to do it anywhere, from a cabin in the desert to a city high-rise. But just as there are many definitions of happiness there are also various definitions of simple, sustainable, green living, as Duane Elgin points out.

From there, we go on to consider some of the general principles of living green and then to examine certain specific aspects, such as food, bodily fitness, the link between simplicity and spirituality and also the nature of activism.

THREE MEDIA VIEWS OF
GREEN LIVING

Duane Elgin

I t is ironic that green ways of living that emphasize voluntary
simplicity – a life-way that can take us into an opportunity-filled
future – are often portrayed in the mass media as regressive ways of
life that turn away from progress. Here are three portrayals of green
lifestyles and simplicity common in today's popular media:

1. Crude or Regressive Simplicity

The mainstream media often shows simplicity as a path of regress
instead of progress. Simplicity is frequently presented as anti-
technology and anti-innovation, a backward-looking way of life
that seeks a romantic return to a bygone era. Profiles often depict
a utopian, back-to-nature movement with families leaving the
stresses of an urban life in favor of living in the woods, or on a farm,
or in a recreational vehicle, or on a boat. Often it is a stereotypical
view of a crudely simple lifestyle – a throwback to an earlier time
and more primitive condition – with no indoor toilet, no phone, no
computer, no television, and no car. No thanks! Seen in this way,
simplicity is a cartoon lifestyle that seems naive, disconnected, and
irrelevant – an approach to living that can be easily dismissed as
impractical and unworkable. Regarding simplicity as regressive and
primitive makes it easier to embrace a 'business as usual' approach
to living in the world.

2. Cosmetic or Superficial Simplicity

In recent years, a different view of simplicity has begun to appear:

a cosmetic simplicity that attempts to cover over deep defects in our modern ways of living by giving the appearance of meaningful change. Shallow simplicity assumes that green technologies – such as fuel-efficient cars, fluorescent light bulbs, and recycling – will fix our problems, give us breathing room, and allow us to continue pretty much as we have in the past without requiring that we make fundamental changes in how we live and work. Cosmetic simplicity puts green lipstick on our unsustainable lives to give them the outward appearance of health and happiness. A superficial simplicity gives a false sense of security by implying that small measures will solve great difficulties. A cosmetic simplicity perpetuates the status quo by assuming that, with use of green technologies we can moderate our impact and continue along our current path of growth for another half century or more.

3. Deep or Conscious Simplicity

Occasionally presented in the mass media and poorly understood by the general public is a conscious simplicity that represents a deep, graceful, and sophisticated transformation in our ways of living – the work that we do, the transportation that we use, the homes and neighborhoods in which we live, the food that we eat, the clothes that we wear, and much more. A sophisticated and graceful simplicity seeks to heal our relationship with the earth, with one another, and with the sacred universe. Conscious simplicity is not simple. This life way is growing and flowering with a garden of expressions. Deep simplicity fits aesthetically and sustainably into the real world of the 21st century.

Few people would voluntarily go through the difficulty of fundamentally restructuring their manner of living and working if they thought they could tighten their belts and wait for things to return to 'normal.' A majority of people will shift their ways of living only when it is unmistakably clear that we must make dramatic and lasting changes. Has the world reached a point of no return and crossed a threshold where a shift toward the simple prosperity of green lifestyles is the new 'normal'?

* * *

This short essay originally appeared as a blog post in the Huffington Post in 2011 and is reprinted here with permission.

Duane Elgin is the well-known author of *Voluntary Simplicity: Toward a Way of Life That Is Outwardly Simple, Inwardly Rich* (first published in 1981, with a Second Edition, published by Harper in 2010) and *The Living Universe: Where Are We? Who Are We? Where Are We Going?* (Berrett-Koehler 2009).

THE GREAT PARADOX OF SIMPLICITY

Marian Van Eyk McCain

When you actually stop to think about it, simplicity is far from being a simple subject. In fact, as I set out on my journey to explore exactly what is 'the simple life,' the first thing I met, sitting like a boulder in the middle of the road, was a huge paradox.

It dawned on me that if you look at the average person in an average house in an average town or village in the Western world, living an average sort of life, you realise that the life he or she lives is quite complex. There are bills to be paid, timelines to be adhered to, obligations to meet, money to earn, taxes to figure out, cars to drive, a household to maintain, a lawn to mow. There are washing machines that break down, kids who get sick, marriages that go on the rocks, tyres that go flat, and fleas on the cat. Dealing with the demands of an ordinary life is no simple matter.

Which, I suppose, is why so many people dream of escaping to something simpler, more basic, more peaceful. A little cottage in the country, perhaps. Or even something on a Greek island, far away from traffic and pollution and the relentless nine-to five slog and the twice daily commute with all the other wage slaves.

But when you look more closely, you find that, in fact, the average life that I just described is, in many ways, the simpler option. Just as you can drive your car through traffic without spending much mental energy on what your hands and feet are doing, so can you live that average sort of life without having to think for yourself a whole lot. At the supermarket you can buy prepared meals to heat up in the microwave. Insurance – for yourself, your house, your health, your pets, your possessions – takes care of the worry about unexpected expenses that may arise from catastrophe. TV provides your entertainment, newspapers keep you informed. The school educates your children and your favourite mechanic looks after your car – which has cruise control for long drives. Your bills go on direct debit, your employer pays your salary straight into your bank, and your money is available at the touch of an ATM. Labour-saving devices do your housework, central heating keeps you warm and double glazing keeps out the noise. And when it is holiday time, a travel agent will find you a package tour that includes everything, so all you have to do is lie on the beach and turn pink.

Holidays, in fact, are a good example of the paradox. Ask people to describe what would be the most simple, basic, no-frills holiday they can think of, and they will probably say a camping trip. Yet if you have ever planned and organised a camping trip you will know that a package tour to Spain – or even Africa – is really a much simpler option, at least for you, if not for the folks who set it up for you.

So 'The Simple Life,' as most people imagine it, is not necessarily less trouble to live, or less trouble to organise. In fact it will probably take more planning, more thinking about and quite a lot more effort to live than the average, mainstream sort of lifestyle that most people have, in the same way that choosing dinner from the a la carte menu takes more energy and forethought than saying "I'll have the set meal, please."

There is really no difference between the package tour and the camping trip, because in each case someone has to organise it all. It is just that with the package tour, that part is hidden. From your point of view, it is a question of pay your money, collect your vouchers, tie on your luggage labels and go.

In the same way, the ready-to-eat meal you buy in the supermarket has been cooked and assembled by someone, somewhere, albeit on factory scale rather than in a home kitchen. What is hidden from you is not only those people's labour but the labour of the people who made the plastic container it comes in, the labour of the people who made the plastic that the container is made of, the lorry that transported both the food and the containers to the factory and then the completed dish from factory to supermarket. And then there is the labour of the people who made the lorry and all its components and the people who dug the oil wells to get the oil that made the petrol for the lorry (and the plastic for the container) ... and on and on it goes, like 'The house that Jack built.' All that complexity is totally hidden from us. The simplicity of being able to buy that meal and heat it up is paid for, if you like, by the huge – but hidden – complexity of that meal's creation. So if we seek that other kind of simplicity – the simplicity of the camping trip, the home made bread and home grown vegetables from the garden – we have to take most of that complexity back on to ourselves.

In the same way that the complexity that goes into creating the supermarket meal is hidden from us, so is the true cost. Hidden away out of sight in a supermarket banana, a bag of coffee beans or a cheap shirt is the cost of the fuel it took to get them all there and the cost in human misery and poverty experienced by growers in far-off lands who get paid a pittance for their produce, and the workers who toil in sweatshops or get sick and die from pesticides in plantations and cotton fields.

So what I have realised (not in one, glorious 'aha' moment but over a number of years of exploring all this), is that if I want to live in a way that removes me from the guilt of supporting all that, then my life is destined to become, in certain ways, more complex, rather than more simple. The Way of Least Resistance is the way that feels simple. The Way of Consciousness, followed by most of the people whose lifestyles we admire as 'simple,' does not always feel as simple on the inside as it looks on the outside. That is the paradox I discovered.

The commonsense way to deal with this big boulder of paradox is to think about trade-offs. Because there is always a trade-off between convenience and time/energy. Most of the conveniences we have come to take for granted in our twenty-first century world cost time and energy, but it is usually someone else's time and energy. So when my partner and I moved to our thirty acres in the mountains of south-eastern Australia in 1993 and started creating a home there, we had very few conveniences at all – except a car and small caravan. We built a shed, with a tank next to it, and caught rainwater from the shed roof. Our first toilet was a hole in the ground. Later, we built a composting toilet. Our time and energy was mostly spent, during those early months, on providing for ourselves the basic necessities which we had taken for granted in the city – a roof over our heads, (first a wooden cabin, then a mudbrick house) water to drink, sanitation, light (first candles, then a paraffin lamp, then later, solar panels), heating and cooking facilities (first a fire, then a woodstove and a solar oven). So we had almost zero convenience at first, and were using almost all our time and energy taking care of our own, basic needs – the ones at the lowest level of Maslow's famous pyramid of needs.

As time went on, we created more convenience. With the solar power, once again we had light at the flick of a switch – and so on. Eventually, we reached the point where we felt perfectly balanced. We were still living close to the Earth, getting pleasure from growing and preparing our food, baking bread in our stove, composing almost all our waste and putting it back to nourish the soil, drawing energy from the sun and living far from the noise and pressure of city life. But we had created enough convenience that we now had time and energy left over for other things. We had reached our point of equilibrium, and it felt just right.

Not everyone will achieve equilibrium in as radical a way as we did – by scrapping everything and starting again from scratch. Most would not be able to – and neither would we, had we done it earlier in our lives, with dependent children and no savings. So for most people, simplifying is more a matter of working backwards towards equilibrium, by keeping most of the conveniences one already has, dispensing with a few, and thinking carefully before investing in any more. If you already have a lawn-mower that works (even though you have to pull the cord six times to get it started) why would you need to swap it for a posher version? Maybe it would be better to save the money and simply spend the time and energy pulling that cord. When it finally conks out, you could downsize to an old-fashioned hand mower and get more exercise.

Then again, if your children are grown up and no-one needs the lawn to play ball or do handstands on any more, why not invest a little time and energy into converting the lawn to a mini-woodland of shrubs and small trees with a floor of pine bark mulch and some nice boulders? Then you would have created some more habitat for the birds and other creatures, and never have to mow again. What could be more convenient than that?

Some of the trade-offs I discovered in my various versions of the simple life have been in the 'lesser of two evils' category. Those are often hard to figure out. For instance, the chemicals in re-chargeable batteries are deadlier than the ones in the disposables, but the former last heaps longer. So it is better to have more of the less deadly chemicals or fewer of the more deadly ones? Coal is the most efficient fuel for our old Rayburn stove in the kitchen, but it has to be trucked two hundred miles from the coal mine and it makes a mess, is heavy to cart around in the coal bucket and the soot in the air is bad for my asthma. Oil would be the cheapest fuel, and has no polluting smoke, but that comes from many more hundreds of miles – and the stove would need converting or replacing. Wood is the most local, but the more wood is collected, the less habitat for the other creatures who depend on old logs and fallen trees and the fewer nutrients are left to return to the soil. Besides which, it burns faster than coal so we need more of it. Best of all, so far, seems to be the idea of pellets made from sawdust, which are a by-product of sawmills. Especially if a local supply-chain can be established, which I'm told is likely to happen soon. However, that option, too, like oil, will probably involve replacing the stove. So now we have to factor in all the energy which goes into creating the new stove and the materials it's made of, and balance that against the energy we are saving by not using coal or oil. Over time, converting to pellets may work out to be the best option. But when the time comes that all the electricity on the grid comes from wind, tide, sunshine or biofuel, then the equation will change again and we shall find ourselves weighing the energy cost of new, heating appliances against the benefits of clean, smokeless air.

Like this, many of the trade-offs which pop up along the road to simplicity are difficult ones, constantly shifting and changing as new information and new factors come in. And one may not always make the best or perfect choice. Sometimes, there is no perfect choice. But the important thing is this: by stopping each time to consider all the pros and cons of where you are going and why, you will be doing something many people are not yet able to do: taking responsibility for the dilemmas of the Earth.

Not that you are solving them. How could you do that, single-handed? But we are all shouldering our share of the burden, simply by thinking about the issues, considering the pros and cons of each decision, and taking what feels to us, after due consideration, the best and most eco-friendly way forward that we can manage at this point. That is perhaps the most significant and important step we shall make on this journey – picking up the burden of our share and doing the best we can to carry it. Since many hands, as we know, make light work, if every man and woman on Earth would just do that, all our planet's seemingly intractable environmental problems would soon melt in the warmth of humanity's universal care and concern.

*   *   *

This chapter is adapted from *The Lilypad List: 7 Steps to the Simple Life*, published by Findhorn Press in 2004.

LIFE ON THE ALLOTMENT
Chris Holmes

What follows is an update of an essay I wrote ten years ago describing my early days tending an allotment. I am happy to say that my wife Jill and I have kept at it and that it remains a great joy and place of learning – and much hard work.

Introduction

When I was a young man, commuting by train to London and working inside an office for five days a week seemed an entirely normal state of affairs. My father did it and so did most of my friends. Looking back to those days of the late 1960's and 1970's, I sensed that I had a strong desire to be outdoors and away from concrete but this seemed to be about the need to engage in sporting activity, mainly of the competitive kind. Running, tennis and hill walking holidays, with the natural world as background, satisfied this need and it took a long time for Nature to come to the foreground, for me to realise that it was the immersion in Nature that left me most fulfilled rather than the sport.

Strangely, this transformation was largely due to a shift in my understanding of my own body. I had thought of it as a machine which I tried to keep well oiled; I was an excellent example of body-mind dualism. For reasons I cannot now remember I began to read about the Eastern disciplines and some of the less well known Western counterparts. I began to make connections with my own body and as I felt more 'at home' in my own space so my relationship with the natural world began to deepen – though I was still very much at the shallow end of the pool. As I immersed myself more deeply in ecological matters I realised that something was missing; that something was a practical, active engagement, a need to get my hands 'dirty'. Jill was way ahead of me in gardening matters and suggested that an allotment might be the answer so with her encouragement, and with the disbelief of others, I made enquiries at my local council offices.

Early Days

The site which was allocated to us is fairly close to home and one of the most attractive and secluded in the London Borough of Sutton. Situated on a bend in the River Wandle, it is enclosed on two sides by a high brick wall and is open to the river on the other. Part of the site is given over to wildlife. When we arrived a rare moth – the currant clearwing – was the star inhabitant, but this is no longer seen. After parting with the modest annual rental, a new phase of living began. The early months (it was late Autumn 2004) involved a good deal of hard work, preparing some neglected and quite difficult ground. By February, sufficient had been cleared to allow the planting of broad bean seeds… So it progressed over the following months, planning, digging, composting and planting, watering and watching with amazement at the extraordinary growth of beautiful vegetables. Not all were successful, but by the late autumn of 2005 the overall harvest had been truly bountiful. The joy of eating one's own freshly picked produce is surely one of life's delights, and this indeed was the only purpose I had in mind in the early days. But I was soon to discover that there was a great deal more to allotments than meets the eye.

Laundry First…

Some years ago I read a wonderful book by the Buddhist author Jack Kornfield. After the Ecstasy, the Laundry has a title which, hopefully, is self explanatory. Mostly life seems to be about the laundry, and the allotment has plenty of it. What came as a huge surprise was the ecstasy. To deal with the laundry first, in the context of an allotment this largely consists of a mix of physical discomfort along with some modest psychological pressure. The discomfort arises from sometimes working in harsh weather, although those of us with masochistic tendencies can transform this into triumph over adversity (however, lower back pain, an occasional intruder, certainly cannot be made pleasurable!) The pressure arises in those spring and summer months during which one is working hard to keep up with Nature's extraordinary pace. The almost constant need to weed, water and deal in an ethical way with predators can result in an obsessive need to visit one's allotment every day – perhaps one might call it vegetable care disorder. Away from the allotment, one occasionally meets people who express incomprehension or surprise at your activities. If one is in the right mood it can be a great opportunity to explain and evangelise about the benefits and joys of organic gardening – though a gift of veg is more likely to produce conversion.

….and the Ecstasy

Sitting at my computer on a dull winter day I am reconsidering the word 'ecstasy.' It feels too strong for my English sensibilities. 'Joy' is closer, though this word reminds me of what evangelical Christians have promised if I would only turn to Jesus. With apologies for compartmentalising a blessing so seamless, here is my list of allotment joys which include some ecstatic moments.

First, working in the open air. With so much of one's life having been spent indoors, whether at school or in an office, time given to the allotment has provided a revelatory experience. Sometimes uncomfortable and challenging, allotment work engenders a deep sense of coming home. A recapitulation of our evolutionary path, or maybe the fact that the vast majority of my ancestors up until the 20th century were farming people…who knows? What I am sure of is that working within the felt context of earth, air and water (the river, along with its inhabitants, is a constant part of my environment) as well as the occasional fire (not forgetting the sun) feels so at home and deeply pleasurable.

Second, the joy of working with one's body in new ways. Years of running and gym work provided me a good physical base but I found that the constant mix of bending, carrying, kneeling, lifting, squatting and stretching bestowed a novel collection of sensations. Over time I found that if I moved mindfully I could engage in a more purposeful bodywork, 'a green gym' I suppose. Just as movement is often a source of joy, so to is non-movement. A spell of hard work followed by a pause in activity, the quiet inspection of one's achievements, followed by observation of the wider scene, then a return to work – this fundamental rhythm of gardening always engenders good feelings within.

Third, the joy of cooperation with the natural world. I once read that spiritual awakening occurs at that point in life where you begin to make friends with not being able to control everything. Life on the allotment soon tests any desire to control or dominate Nature, but change one's mindset into one of cooperation and life becomes far more interesting and satisfying. The gardener certainly has an important role to play but it is always contributory, something our food industry has long forgotten.

Fourth, growing one's own food is very empowering. This feels like an overused word, but no other comes to mind. The sense of achievement, of being creative, self-reliant (in the context of cooperation with Nature), and journeying from almost total ignorance to modest expertise gives great satisfaction. Perhaps the most powerful of these is the feeling of removing oneself (partly at least) from the vast industrial/corporate web of food production and consumption into a more natural web of people who work to sustain the Earth through organic agriculture and Permaculture.

Fifth, community and communion. It is very satisfying to work alongside other people on an allotment site. Their thoughts may be closed to you but their actions are visible and often funny; allotments seem to encourage idiosyncratic behaviour and eccentric physical constructions. Life for agricultural workers in the old days may have been very hard, but one of the compensations must surely have been the joy of communal work. The exchange of produce between allotment holders and the gifts of vegetables to family and friends have a richness which gifts purchased with money do not. There is also a joy in non-ownership. Working on and paying rent for an allotment 'owned' by the local council lacks the ties which come from owning the land, and feels part of an old-fashioned public ethic which is fast disappearing.

Sixth, hospitality. The allotment sees many types of visitor including, it is important to remember, oneself. In recent weeks the robin has been prominent, along with swans and ducks on the adjacent river. Soon there will be a host of creatures eager to share in the feast, whether vegetable or animal. While I would love to welcome them all, some clearly have an agenda which conflicts with mine! Some you have to deter and remove, otherwise you lose your crops. Maybe the best piece of advice is that which was given to me while working on an organic farm in France some time back – always leave some for the others.

The Present Moment

Allotments are good for developing the contemplative within. The mix of work, stepping back and stopping to reflect seems congruent with our human make-up and with the great wisdom traditions. Things happen unexpectedly. One day in spring years ago – I cannot recall what I was doing – I awoke from whatever was absorbing me to a sense of being totally present to myself and in complete harmony with everything surrounding me. As a poor meditator who had talked a lot about the virtues of being in the here and now, but who was mostly somewhere else in time, I was mightily pleased with this graced moment. There have been others since. So, fellow seekers of the present moment, do not despair. Take up the fork and wheelbarrow...

Future

It is ten years since I began my allotment life, and my early enthusiasm remains though of a different quality. Though I have experienced a great deal I realise how little I really know and understand of horticulture. The regular comment of my old school reports drift into my consciousness: 'Must do better'. As for the spiritual dimension, these are my words from a decade ago:

'I was considering calling this essay "The spiritual dimension of the allotment" but this seemed over the top and premature. Perhaps five years more work may give the title some legitimacy. I feel I must continue to dig on this spiritual ground, in the sure and certain knowledge that there are more connections to be made, more joys, more ecstasy and, of course a lot of laundry.'

I am afraid that I can only humbly repeat myself. There is much work to do!

*   *   *

Chris Holmes has been a member of GreenSpirit for 17 years, is a past Chair and a long-serving member of Council. He has spent the past two decades unlearning the effects of 30 years of working in the world's stock markets. The original essay was first published in The GreenSpirit Journal in 2006.

HEALTHY PLANET
– HEALTHY BEINGS
Sky McCain

*A new scientific truth does not triumph by convincing its opponents
and making them see the light, but rather because its opponents
eventually die, and a new generation grows up that is familiar with it.*
– Max Planck.

Earth is what we all have in common.
– Wendell Berry.

The other day, weeding the spot where last year's runner beans
had grown, I found a fallen bean that had started to sprout.
Already there were little pink nitrogen nodules clinging to its tiny
roots and the sight of them took me instantly back to my days in
Australia, working to fill our thirty acres of over-grazed land with
new trees. One of the important lessons I learned was that in order
to ensure survival of nitrogen-hungry eucalypt species, one should
first plant lots of fast growing but short-lived wattle trees. These
take nitrogen from the air, accumulate it on their roots and release
it into the soil when they die.

This interdependence of living organisms, this beautiful
symbiosis that we find happening everywhere we look in Nature
is, according to the late Lynn Margulis, every bit as basic to life
on Earth as the random genetic mutations theorised by Charles
Darwin. Gaia, our planet, wastes nothing, recycles everything. Over
and over we find that the waste from one organism is food for
another. Interdependence is a basic law of Nature.

Organic farmers and vegetable growers know this, which is why they use methods like crop rotation, composting, companion planting and so on. It is a well-proven fact that organic growing methods and the avoidance of pesticides, GMOs, irradiation or chemical fertilisation, strengthens the health of both the soil and the crops and frequently improves yields. It is also beyond doubt that organically produced food is the healthiest option for all creatures, including humans. To be healthy we need healthy food and to grow healthy food we rely on that great bed of nurturing fertility on the Earth's crust that we call soil. We need that soil to be healthy because we have learned a lot about how healthy plants grow out of healthy soil. We must also keep in mind that our metabolic regulatory patterns were formed from our environment as we evolved. Thus, it behoves us to study, insofar as possible, the environmental components that influenced our evolution. It is often said that we are what we eat. The nutritional value of what we put in our mouths is paramount in maintaining a healthy body and depends wholly on the quality of our environment. Yet something has gone badly wrong. What has gone wrong and why?

Humans have significantly altered the face of our planet Earth. In North America alone, the Great Plains prairie once spread across 560,000 square miles (that's a little over twice the size of Texas!) but less than 2% of native prairie remains today. Nearly one third of the world's arable topsoil has been lost over the last forty years at a rate of over ten million hectares yearly. It can take from five hundred to one thousand years to build an inch of topsoil. In many areas, desertification has destroyed topsoil permanently. During all the hours spent on my knees planting trees on those rocky hillsides I was constantly aware of how desperately thin the Australian topsoil was and how the thoughtless importation of European farming methods into such a different ecosystem had worsened the problem in the last two centuries.

As we learned from the Gaia Theory formulated by Lovelock and Margulis, Gaia has been able to regulate temperature, atmospheric content and many other factors, including soil, to stay healthy. When we fail to observe this and ignore Gaia's modus operandi, we endanger all life. So why do most farmers continue to deplete the fertility of the soil and make it so much harder to produce healthy food?

There is no simple answer. Claiming that farmers are greedy is not a good place to start. A reasonable starting point might be with the realisation that we are strongly conditioned by our culture's language. In our minds, 'Nature' and 'Earth' have been separated. We learn that 'Nature' refers to all living things outside of ourselves that the Earth is a lump of rock that we live 'on'. Thus we grow up with the illusion that:

1. We are not part of Nature, and...

2. Although Nature is alive the Earth is not.

Many of us talk about how deeply we feel connected to Nature. But this doesn't go far enough. Our observations that we are 'connected' to the Earth are valid, but connectedness paints a fairly dim image of our relationship to Gaia and obscures its fundamental truth. In fact, we, Nature and Earth are all one and the same. The truth is that we do not just live ON Gaia, we ARE Gaia.

Consider a tree. We use our thinking function to subdivide a tree into parts such as leaves, trunk and roots. But referring to the leaves, for instance, does not negate the fact that the leaves are the tree. The trunk and roots are also the tree. To say that the leaves are connected to the tree obscures the fact that the leaves are the tree. To say that my hand or arm is connected to me obscures the fact that all my parts are me.

We see ourselves as advanced, self-organising living beings and most of us also consider ourselves to be conscious beings. Yet although we are entirely dependent on Gaia for our health and survival and our very existence, we often fail to appreciate that our planet itself is a living, self-organising organism, even more so than we are. We need to recognise that the wondrous beauty, diversity, and life-supporting qualities of Gaia are not due to dumb luck or the result of random shakes of cosmic dice. Gaia has a development and maintenance system that we must examine from the realisation that using machine-checking instruments to probe what we view as dead matter will inevitably result in further destructive behaviour. The carbon cycle is a good example of one of the many ways in which our planet exhibits self-organizing and self-sustaining behaviour. By interfering with that, we have created problems that at best will stretch Gaia's healing abilities to the utmost and at worst could totally change the shape of life as we know it.

A further obstacle to working in a way that is healing for us and all life forms and the planet is our anthropocentric outlook which sanctions governments to treat Gaia like a vast cookie tin with a label on the top that says "for humans only". We are egocentric and not ecocentric in our outlook on land use. Again, our use of words such as 'resources', or phrases like 'ecosystem services' constantly reinforces the view that Gaia is simply a source of wealth for humans only.

Once we truly understand that we are the Earth, that the Earth is a living, conscious being and that it is NOT all about us; we shall surely recognise that our health and Gaia's health are not just connected but utterly intertwined, joined and interdependent. They are one and the same. Our healing and the wellbeing of all life are dependent on Gaia's healing. Neither we nor any other living organism can be healthy unless Gaia is healthy.

So what can we individuals do? So much of the environmental destruction we read about is caused by forces beyond our ability to influence. However, taking an interest and supporting the production of clean local food is a realisable goal for every single one of us. The higher the demand for organic, locally grown food, the more the market will respond and the more the farming sector will be encouraged to turn to decentralized and diversified farming practices that naturally boost soil health and farm resilience. These include: crop rotations, cover crops, reducing tillage where it makes sense, and building local food systems. We all need to encourage our local food stores to accept nutritious locally produced food.

Recently, a food survey conducted by Oklahoma State University found that: more than three-quarters of the consumers polled said adopting a more 'natural' agricultural production system – that includes additional local, organic and unprocessed foods – would be most effective at addressing the future food challenges rather than adopting a more 'technological' agricultural system.[1]

And we can plant seeds. Even if it is just a container on the windowsill or a planter on a balcony, we can all grow something to eat. This year, I shall plant my runner beans in a different spot to maximise the health of the soil in my garden. Knowing that the more local my food is to my bioregion the lower its carbon footprint, I shall be shopping once again at the farmers market. Every little helps when you want to become a healthy planet.

*   *   *

Reference:

1. Science, New Series, Vol. 267, No. 5201 (Feb. 24, 1995) 1117-1123.

Sky McCain, an American citizen living in Devon, is the author of *Planet as Self: An Earthen Spirituality* (Earth Books, 2011). He likes walking, playing the trombone in his local brass band, and visiting his favourite parts of southern Europe. Sky graduated from Boston College in the US and has an MA in Values in the Environment from Lancaster University, UK. He has also been involved in 'green' activism in the local community and was the co-founder of the Wholesome Food Association, an organization that champions local food.

THE GREEN GYM: GREEN EXERCISE AND GREEN FITNESS

Chris Holmes

I want to show that exercise in natural surroundings is 'good for you' and also better, in the long run, than in the conventional modern indoor gym. The 'green gym', 'green exercise' and 'green fitness' are terms that are often used interchangeably but in this essay I use them with distinct, if overlapping meanings. By the 'green gym' I mean a high intensity workout undertaken where natural surroundings are dominant; a half hour training session in one's back garden or an effortful 5 or 10 kilometre run in the local park would qualify as examples. 'Green exercise' is broader in scope and, while embracing the 'green gym' also includes walking, mountain biking, wild swimming, gardening, maybe horse riding; essentially any outdoor pursuits undertaken in a non-competitive mode primarily for enjoyment and with Nature a dominant feature. 'Green fitness' is a more holistic concept which includes green exercise but also nutrition, rest and various forms of support such as massage therapies and complementary medicine. It also goes beyond individual well being and considers the wider interaction with society and with the Earth.

The 'State of the Art' Gym

The room before me is vast, lit entirely by artificial light, with not a window to be seen nor any hint of the natural world. An array of machines of various shapes, sizes and functions decorate the floor; bodies of various shapes, sizes and ages are performing a range of movements – walking, running, stepping, pushing, pulling, rowing, cycling, stretching. On the far side of the room is the free weights area inhabited mainly by over-muscled young men. On the near side is a high intensity floor class, an update of the traditional circuit training which I remember as a teenager and with far more noise. On the wall facing the running and biking machines stands a huge digital clock, below which are eight giant TV screens. The 'music' is continuous, loud, repetitive and frankly awful.

While most people are training with varying degrees of intensity, some are talking to each other, others are talking or texting on their phones. Those narcissistically inclined are looking into the mirrors which line the walls, which allow one to observe not only oneself but much of the rest of the gym population, a sort of 21st century version of Jeremy Bentham's panopticon. Some have no hesitation in displaying their form in designer gear – these are generally younger people – others, usually older people, tend to cover up a little. Old, in this place, is over fifty.

This gym has a 'pecking order', depending on the time of day and the part of the gym one is working in. In the free weights area, muscle size is the key determinant in one's positioning; on the running and biking machines the slender bodies are supreme. In the high intensity floor classes the combination of strength, agility and stamina requires a muscular litheness. On entering gym space your physical status is rapidly assessed via direct gaze or by mirror and you are – consciously or unconsciously – allocated to a level in the hierarchy of physical capability and, it should be said, attractiveness. If one is towards or at the bottom of the pile then all is not lost, for one may be spotted by a 'personal trainer' and soon (if one can afford it) be on the road to transformation.

This then is the modern gym, at least one example of it, a palace where technology and consumer capitalism meet with the quests for body enhancement and the efficient use of one's time. There is just a hint here of the old fashioned factory and 'music while you work'. A recapitulation of the manual labour which was once the norm. It's energy guzzling, unnatural and expensive, like much of modernity.

Maybe this is too harsh a judgement on this 'state of the art' gym, for it undoubtedly has some positive aspects for the individual, if not for society or the wider Earth. First, these modern gyms provide convenience and relative comfort, particularly during the dark days of winter when even the most dedicated and hardy green fitness enthusiast may find it difficult or sometimes impossible to exercise outside.

Second, gyms are good for certain specialisations. If you are seeking strength, power and size – which many young men are – then the equipment and progression provided in a conventional gym is hard to replicate in a natural environment.

Third, one might find more of a community within the confines of the local gym than in the often less hospitable environment outside. This may also mean peer pressure to perform – sometimes good, sometimes not.

For the individual therefore there are indeed positive features to offset against the negative. What I find annoying however is the assumption among many that the modern gym is the best, the natural place to get fit. So often I have heard someone say that they want to lose weight or get into shape, and have therefore 'joined the local gym'. This seems to me an often unconsidered and blinkered choice. In this essay I hope to show that the overall health of the individual, society and the Earth is better served by 'green exercise' – and specifically by the 'green gym' – which can provide very cheaply an excellent range of physical movement and the possibility of exploring a spiritual dimension sourced by the natural world and our own intimate part of Nature, our bodies.

Green Gym, Green Exercise and Green Fitness

Feeling good in one's body is surely an important ingredient in human flourishing, necessary but by no means sufficient. While human 'wholeness', creativity, wisdom and fulfilment have often co-existed with less than ideal and sometimes wretched physicality, it is surely the case that most of us do better when we are feeling fit and well. However, fitness is a word with a wide range of meaning. The statement that someone is 'fit' can encompass a variety of body types, body mass indices, ages and heart rates. Then there is the question of fitness for what; in competitive sport the fitness of a rugby player will be somewhat different from that of a cricketer or distance runner; in everyday life, the gardening enthusiast may be 'fit' in a way the walking enthusiast is not. In order to avoid writing a lengthy preamble I shall make the assumption that we can accept a broad definition, that we know roughly what fitness is and that a key ingredient is exercise – by which I mean movement which raises our heart rate, requires effort, possibly causes breathlessness and which creates some discomfort (though not pain). When combined with sufficient rest and a balanced diet, exercise improves not only our physical health but also our self confidence and self discipline. It can also be helpful in the area of mental health which I will discuss later.

The 'green gym' I define as a training session of between twenty minutes and an hour in natural surroundings which, if undertaken regularly over several months and with sufficient intensity, will rapidly promote fitness. Green gym workouts might include the following:

Running, speed walking or biking in parkland, urban common land, countryside and wilderness.

A mixed training routine – perhaps running plus 'calisthenics' – in the same surroundings as above. Many public parks now have fitness trails and exercise areas with equipment.

A training session containing a variety of strength, power, flexibility and stability exercises in one's own garden, maybe using equipment. There is great deal of second hand equipment for sale. Speed gardening – basically working as hard and fast as you can – on one's garden or allotment. This has the virtue of accomplishing a task or series of tasks as well as aiding fitness.

Using green space for disciplines such as yoga or tai chi. These tend to have slower, more controlled movements, but can be just as demanding as the mix of press-ups, squats, sit-ups, pull-ups, bent over twists, dead lifts and whatever else one might incorporate in a more traditional western style workout.

'Green exercise' is broader in scope and while embracing the green gym would also include such popular activities as country walking, mountain biking, gardening, and minority pursuits such as 'wild' swimming, river/sea canoeing and rock climbing. These are activities which many of us participate in; there are millions who garden in this country and significant numbers who walk in the countryside. Green exercise will differ somewhat from the pure green gym because it will be rather less focused on the goal of fitness and more on enjoyment of the activity. Green exercise can take place in a variety of settings, from wild mountain terrain to the domestic garden. Most of us live in urban or suburban areas and parkland will inevitably be our main green context.

My own experience is worth recounting. I happen to live in an outer London suburb, heavily populated with extremely busy roads but within half a mile there is extensive parkland and common ground. The River Wandle flows close by and one can walk, run or cycle for several miles along its course. Running and walking in green space is therefore relatively straightforward although the terrain is somewhat flat and undemanding. I am also fortunate enough to have an allotment and a smallish garden which allows for alternatives to running and walking. The Surrey Hills are half an hour distant by train or car. My point is that nearly everyone in this country can find places near to them for green exercise; it's a matter of doing some homework, maybe with an ordnance survey map. If you are a town dweller, become a psycho-geographer – just go walking and make discoveries of green routes and green space on your doorstep.

'Green fitness' is a holistic concept, including as it does green exercise and the green gym, nutrition, rest, massage or bodywork therapies and the various forms of complementary medicine. It also includes a broader and deeper sense of living well, of 'right livelihood', of our relationship with the Earth and the development of an ecological spirituality. Thus green fitness is a very open-ended concept, leading way beyond the narrower bounds of physical movement.

Before leaving this section I think it important to make a brief mention of competitive sport. There are a number of competitive sports which are played outside in green space; every weekend my local park is host, depending on the season, to cricket, tennis, football and occasionally cross country racing. Not too far away there is a golf course – which I confess to having some qualms about. I am fully supportive of these sports, particularly my own love, tennis. However, the 'green' element is nearly always the context rather than the focus. The very nature of competition, with the quality of concentration required and the range of emotions involved lead me to conclude that under most circumstances, sport cannot be classified as green exercise.

Not so long ago I competed in a 10 kilometre 'trail' race through Surrey heathland which, if walked at a moderate or slow pace, would have been delightful. All I remember, however, was discomfort with the effort involved, that the natural surroundings were there to be negotiated rather than enjoyed and that my main desire was simply to finish in a reasonable time. The environment was very much in the background. Such competitive activities definitely have a value, for we benefit greatly from testing ourselves, taking stock of our fitness, feeling the exhilaration of completing a difficult task – and simply feeling the movement of our bodies. It is not, however, green exercise. Furthermore, the upper professional reaches of sport involving extraordinary levels of physical, mental and emotional achievement have little to do with green exercise. The ecological dimension is hard to spot, the benefit to society certainly debatable..

The Benefits of Green Exercise

Why should exercise in natural surroundings be better than exercise in an enclosed space? I discuss the benefits under three main headings:

1. Benefits for the individual
2. Benefits for society and the Earth
3. Developing a contemplative green spirituality

Benefits for the Individual

The writer and academic C.S. Lewis wrote a book entitled 'Surprised by Joy', and this is the perfect phrase to describe some of my own experiences of training in places where natural surroundings are dominant. Joyful experiences do not happen every day – much of the time one dwells in the mundane and repetitive – but as I grow older they seem to happen with increasing frequency; one learns over time to experience joy in the unremarkable. Whether it be the sun rising on my early morning run, a particular pattern of clouds, the smell of the land after rain, the sound and then the sight of swans flying overhead, a heron standing silently still in the river, the realisation that one is being watched by a fox, the feel of earth in my hands as I weed a vegetable patch, these simple wonders I now cherish. I remember as a child that Nature seemed full of amazements, but that these seemed to diminish and fade during my teenage years and beyond. Exercise was always important, but mainly with an instrumental or competitive purpose, and Nature got closed out. So, curiously, did my body which graduated to machine status, only needing to be well oiled.

I have an appalling memory of a speech I made in the 1980's to an audience of business colleagues explaining why distance running was important to me. "It improves my productivity" was the gist of my explanation and indeed were the very words I used. This was very sad! One can look after one's body, but still live at a great distance from it. Thankfully, as my body aged and grew 'less efficient', I became familiar with the Eastern disciplines and recovered my childhood affection for 'Earthly' things. The love of Nature and the joy of my body moving within it are with me now in greater depth and meaning than ever before in my life – but it took a while to get there.

My experience today while exercising largely takes place in my own locality, the parkland and common land of the London Borough of Sutton, in many ways nondescript and appallingly congested but with sizeable areas of green space – a legacy of strong local government (which we no longer have) and a millionaire, land-owning priest who wished to keep out the late 19th century developers at all costs ('nimbyism' is not always negative!)

However, if I want 'ecstatic' experiences, then I will more likely find these in wilder country. I am particularly familiar with the North Yorkshire moors and coastline and the Eastern French Pyrenees, and in both these areas there are many more opportunities to experience profound moments of joy, more challenge and tougher exercise. Many of us will have these special places which we love and know to some degree and where there is much still to be discovered. However, most of us spend the major part of our time in 'ordinary' places and it is important to seek out the depths and detail of where we live for otherwise we will live not in the present but in the memorable experiences of the past and expectations of future delights. Worse, we may become collectors of our own adventures which we can recount at length to any unfortunate listeners. I have met such people!

The discussion of exercising in wilder areas reminds me that this is by no means always pleasurable. Exercise itself involves effort, difficulty and discomfort but add in the vagaries of weather and sometimes unpredictable animals and insects and an agreeable session on one's allotment or out walking or running can soon turn sour. I was running on a local path on common land a few days before writing this piece when I received two wasp stings on my left thigh, totally unexpected. Over the decades I have tripped and fallen a few times, been battered by strong winds and hail, been bitten by insects, attacked by dogs, have narrowly avoided being hit by mountain bikes, come across less than friendly hunters with guns, and have become completely lost. Twenty years ago I was running on desert scrubland in Arizona and ran into a knee high cactus. My skin bears the marks to this day! But such incidents are all surely part of the exigencies of life, and green exercise and the green gym will always pose a challenge and a degree of risk, albeit nearly always of a modest nature.

The mention of challenge and risk leads me on to 'freedom'. Sometimes when we say that we feel free we simply mean that it feels good to do what we do. We might also mean the sensation of being open to the elements, being able to see beyond four walls, having space to roam. I feel at my most free when hill walking, where one can see for long distances and where views are frequently changing. A further aspect of freedom is that, compared with everyday life, green exercise is very straightforward. The complexity of work demands, finances, relationships, careers, long and short term plans and goals, all tend to fade from our consciousness when we are focused on a mix of bodily movement and the natural world in which we are immersed. We may begin a country walk, a parkland run or an afternoon on the allotment preoccupied with our concerns, caught up in our own worries, only dimly aware of the sights and sounds of Nature. After a while the rhythm of our activity and the general calmness of the surrounds quietens our mind. Our attention may suddenly be caught by the trilling of a bird, which then appears in view, and then we notice more birds, then the beauty and magnificence of the trees. Our awareness is expanding, roaming across the landscape and slowly we become absorbed in the world around us. Our minds settle into an unaccustomed silence and we feel free from the concerns that preoccupied us earlier. Green exercise immerses us in a greater reality, frees us up and seems to encourage within us a sense of spontaneity, so often lacking in a regulated and demanding society.

Some thirty years ago the evolutionary biologist E.O.Wilson postulated the theory of 'biophilia,' that we humans have an innate emotional affiliation with the natural world. This is superficially an attractive theory but there are many difficulties attached. It certainly remains unproven – if it is capable of proof at all. However, one does not need to agree with the biophilia thesis to propose that we are evolved creatures, part of the great Universe Story and that by far the greater part of our human history has been spent as hunter gatherers. We evolved as creatures living close to or immersed in the natural world and this continued for the majority of us after we settled into a farming existence. Though undoubtedly significant, our species experience of industrialisation and urbanisation is as nothing on the human timeline (and humanity itself is a very recent arrival on Earth). This is not a recommendation that we return to pre-Neolithic ways (though if we continue along our present path we may eventually do so) but it just acknowledges our biology, that we are evolved to walk and run and that our senses are attuned to the natural world – though rather less than they once were. Green exercise recapitulates our ancient past and allows us to feel part of something much bigger, much grander; if nothing else, then four million years of bipedalism gives a context and a mystery to my morning run.

To add a little learning to green exercise, note the creatures that you see and later discover their longevity as a species. Check out the geological age of the land you are on and do a little historical research on the areas in which you exercise – my own allotment site was once the orchard of an 18th century mansion and I often dig up fragments of pottery. The paths and tracks we walk and run on shadow the modern road network and are often ancient; they lead one on, enticing both the eye and the imagination and they hold secrets of adventures and meetings, sadness and joy. As Thomas Hardy put it in 'The Woodlanders,' to belong in a place means "to know all about those invisible ones of the days gone by".

Now to a mundane but very important point which is that green exercise is generally inexpensive. There are some costs involved – good footwear for walking or running is strongly advised (unless one decides to run or walk barefoot – see the article in the summer 2015 GreenSpirit magazine) – and comfortable, suitable clothing also. Gym equipment, if one should decide to purchase some for one's back garden, can easily be acquired second hand. However, green exercise and the green gym will certainly be very much cheaper than one's local conventional gym. It is of course possible to spend a great deal on specialist equipment and clothing. A cursory glance through any of the walking, running or cycling magazines will demonstrate this. But it really is not necessary for fitness; nor, I would suggest, for competitive sport.

Finally, what is the evidence which supports green exercise? Too often the 'green case' loses out to 'big money' because it fails to produce the hard evidence which translates into the conventional money based cost benefit analysis. Some areas of experience are hard to measure, some impossible, and our system is loaded in favour of market interests. This is not so with green exercise. Research on the benefits of exercising in Nature for our physical and mental health have been carried out for several decades and have given support to what we have known for centuries and for what common sense tells us. In recent years the University of Essex, through its 'Green Exercise' Research team has produced a number of psychological research studies which show powerful and conclusive evidence for the beneficial effects of green exercise. These studies are scientific papers and thus require a little more than usual effort in reading but they are available on the Department's website and are well worth accessing.

2. Benefits for Society and the Earth

One of the features which differentiates green fitness from the 'non-green' is its counter-cultural ethos. By this I mean our understanding that our bodies are commercial battlegrounds, fought over by a host of interests, from the largest multinational food company to the smallest hairdressing salon on the high street, and that we have to be alert to what is going on. We have a range of 'body' industries – clothing, cosmetics, cosmetic surgery, drink, fashion, food, hairstyling, jewellery, medicine of every description, nail manicure, pharmaceuticals, slimming, sport to watch and play, tanning, tattooing, and the various modes of exercise. The latter has spawned its own huge industry of gyms, equipment, sportswear, personal trainers, books, bicycles, massage therapists and so on. Most of these industries sub-divide into specialist areas, and each is constituted by a range of enterprises from the large multi-national to the one person operation. Standing behind – or should I say encircling – all this is a huge supporting cast including the media, advertising and retailing. I have no idea what proportion of our gross national product the 'body economy' accounts for but it must be very large indeed.

Try the following. Write your name in the centre of an A4 page and surround your name with the industries that directly make money out of your body. Create a wider circle and behind each industry list the associated organisations (or individuals if appropriate) that you use. It may be difficult to complete the outer circle but list as many organisations and individuals as you can which are involved in your body's maintenance and enhancement. The result may astound you.

Of course, this massive 'body industry' complex is not all bad; there is a world of difference between purveyors of processed junk food and an organic vegetable grower selling local produce in a local market. The important first step – if one takes green fitness seriously – is to be aware of the forces interested in your body and their need to profit from it. It therefore behoves us to look closely at what we purchase and consume and to be as discriminating as we can, ignoring corporate advertising.

When it comes to exercise, choose comfortable clothing and training/running shoes which are ethically produced, and do some research before purchasing. Adjust your diet to a balanced one, keep processed food, ready meals, alcohol and sugary drinks to a minimum, and ensure you get sufficient rest. There is so much good information available (as well as some crackpot ideas) and most of us know what we should be doing. It is not difficult to understand, but in our hyper-consumerist culture it can be a struggle to do. However, with a little effort and persistence, we can all take steps to help not just ourselves but the wider ecology and culture in which we exist. A light footprint on the Earth is the goal, but avoid becoming that rather humourless creature, the green puritan, who will readily indicate where you fall short in your relationship with the environment and who will try and remove pleasures which do not accord with their strict beliefs. Keep a generous heart on your journey; you will ultimately be far more effective in the green cause.

In recent times there has emerged considerable evidence for the beneficial effects of green exercise for various degrees of mental illness. The Care Farming movement, horticulture therapy and various outdoor exercise therapies have demonstrated the impact of green exercise in improving the lives of those with a range of difficulties and disabilities. The concept of 'Nature deficit disorder'(Richard Louv 2009) has done much to alert us to the negative effects of the withdrawal of our children from Nature and natural processes; the epidemics of childhood obesity and attention deficit disorder are closely related to the disconnection between children and the natural world. There is a more insidious impact from technology which derives from the ubiquitous flat screen and which is affecting us all; there is evidence that we are losing our depth perception, that our brains are being remodelled by exposure to digital technology, that electronic screens are changing our consciousness. One critical counter to this trend is surely green exercise which demands the use of the whole body and the encouragement of ecological knowledge rather than ecological ignorance.

3. Developing a Contemplative Green Spirituality

We live in a highly acquisitive society and our culture, filled with the desire to dominate everything in sight, takes great pride in the power of action. In an essay extolling the virtues of physical activity it may seem strange to introduce what is apparently the very opposite, the development of a contemplative, green spirituality, so very counter cultural. Although action and contemplation may seem opposites they are, I believe, profoundly complementary, vitally necessary to each other. Dedication to an active life without the contemplative dimension is a recipe for rootlessness, stress and burnout. Contemplation without the active dimension results in escapism. We need the two poles to interact and we need to try and integrate both into our lives. Green exercise is a wonderful way of celebrating these gifts of life, combining the joy in bodily movement with that of Nature, activity with stepping back and paying deep attention, 'doing' with 'being'.

Many people identify their feelings for the natural world as part of a spiritual longing, a spirituality informed by intimate contact with, and feeling for, the natural. Green exercise can help us to deepen our awareness of existing within the larger whole of the living world, to rethink the fundamental elements of our common existence, to develop what Aldo Leopold named our 'ecological conscience'. By contemplation I do not mean the practice of a technique such as meditation or adopting a particular position, rather any way in which we can look behind the illusions of life, of the sleight of hand practiced by our culture and by our egos to keep us from seeing things as they are. It means cultivating the art of attention in such a way that we can begin to perceive and respond to what Wordsworth called "the life of things". It means engagement with and participation in the natural world, of being attentive to other life-forms, attentive to one's own body in its various movements in Nature. The acquisition of this awareness can be a long and difficult process involving emotional and intellectual 'unlearning' as well as learning but it is a good journey to be on.

Some say that the ultimate experience is that of a dissolution of the boundaries between self and the rest of Nature, a oneness or union. For myself, I recall hardly any occasions of oneness but I do recall many of awe, wonder, harmony and profound attraction, along with a great desire to continue the experience, to not let it go. I am always aware of my difference from other life forms, of the need to appreciate and respect the 'otherness' of the other, while at the same time feeling deeply connected. This has not come easily or quickly to me and I have no doubt that a deep contemplative relationship with Nature may have to be learned and re-learned over a long period. The poet Rainer Maria Rilke wrote about his relationship with Nature thus:

"...it is only very recently that I have gazed at it and savoured it in this way. For a long time we walked along next to each other in embarrassment, nature and I. It was as if I were at the side of a being whom I cherished but to whom I dared not say: 'I love you'. Since then I must have finally said it; I don't know when it was but I feel we have found each other."

– Diaries of a Young Poet.

Just as we need to persevere at gaining fitness in the green gym, so our relationship with Nature will take time to develop. Just as with Rilke, it may take a while for us to say "I love you".

The type of focused and serious attention outlined above may sound like hard work, but there are different types of attention. There is a broad distinction between directed attention, which requires considerable effort and focus by the individual, and reflexive attention, when one's senses are suddenly 'grabbed' or held by something. The particular sound of swans flying overhead, the rapid movement of clouds across the sky, the colour of leaves in the trees, suddenly reaching the brow of a hill and seeing beautiful landscape set out before one, attending to these is well nigh effortless. In the late 1980's Rachel and Stephen Kaplan developed Attention Restoration Theory (ART) which shows that our ability to concentrate or direct our attention can become depleted when having been under a high workload. Their research showed that natural environments are better than most urban settings in undoing such 'directed attention fatigue' because Nature contains many more aesthetically fascinating objects and processes. Such objects and events are effortlessly processed and thus allow other effort-requiring cognitive faculties an opportunity for restoration and recovery.

In a similar vein to ART is the concept of reverie, articulated by Jean-Jacques Rousseau in his *Reveries of a Solitary Walker* written between 1776 and 1778 not long before he died. For Rousseau reverie meant not the absent minded day dreaming which we perhaps normally think of but a form of attentiveness which is spontaneous, where ideas "follow their bent without resistance or constraint", a "pure and disinterested contemplation", a way of contemplating Nature where our passions and practical concerns are in abeyance. As Rousseau puts it:

> ...*reverie amuses and distracts me, thought wearies and depresses me; thinking has always been for me a disagreeable and thankless occupation. Sometimes my reveries end in meditation, but more often my meditations end in reverie. And during these wanderings my soul roams and soars through the universe on the wings of imagination, in ecstasies which surpass all other pleasures.* (Penguin Classics 2004, page 107).

Part of a contemplative spirituality must be healing and in this context it means the healing of our relationship with the Earth. So much damage has been done and is being done by humankind, so much has been lost and is still being lost. We need to be open to grief, to experience lamentation and mourning, and to know how to do it as individuals, as a society and as a species. As Joanna Macy states:

> *Our pain for the world, including the fear, anger, sorrow, and guilt we feel on behalf of the Earth, is not only pervasive. It is natural and healthy. It is dysfunctional only to the extent that it is misunderstood and repressed.*
>
> – *Coming Back to Life*, 1998.

I have been particularly struck by the 4th century Christian desert fathers and their concept and practice of the 'Gift of Tears', an expression not simply of personal loss but a part of a restorative spiritual practice that can reawaken an awareness of the bonds that connect life forms to one another and to the larger ecological whole. Perhaps three words encapsulate this ancient desert way – 'Look, Weep, Live'. If we look long and well enough with a profound attention (at our culpability in the desecration of our planet) then the tears will begin to flow; the tears will have a cleansing effect which will allow us to live responsibly and to act with a renewed intent towards the Earth. This is not a 'one off' – we will look, weep and live many times!

Before concluding this very brief discussion of contemplative green spirituality, there are a couple of aspects of the green gym in particular which need to be highlighted. First, during intensive physical work, our main focus is inevitably on the body – summoning up effort, feeling discomfort, keeping an eye on one's exercise form, feeling energised and flushed by muscular action, considering 'how far to push it', counting the repetitions, and the satisfaction (hopefully) of successful completion. One learns, over time, to listen to the body in a way not given to those who do not experience high intensity training and to bring to the foreground those regions of the body which are, for the most part, absent from our consciousness. There is an incentive to understand, as best we can, the extraordinary processes taking place within; again, to pay deep attention. Second, there is the possibility of becoming lost in intensive physical activity, something the psychologist Mihaly Csikszentmihalyi has called a state of flow, where the experiences of consciousness are in harmony with each other, unlike 'normal' life. Athletes talk of 'being in the zone', religious mystics of being in ecstasy. I must confess that this state seems to happen less frequently as my body ages, but I have certainly known it.

Making a Start

You may already be an experienced green exerciser and understand 'the territory' very well or perhaps this is fairly new. This final section sets out a few tips mainly for those who are starting out on the journey or who perhaps would like to give a deeper consideration to their current efforts.

Body Autobiography

A great way to step back and reflect at any stage on the journey is to write oneself a 'body autobiography'. A couple of pages of A4 will suffice covering subject matter such as the way your family felt about the body and fitness when you were a child your attitude as a teenager, your physical competitiveness, the major body events in your life, the way you feel now. It's best to be brief and not get drawn in too deeply – put the document to one side and return to it in a few months. Take time to really build a considered picture of your history.

An Honest Personal Check and Medical

Stand naked in front of a full length mirror. What do you really see? If possible record your feelings, then do the usual weight, height and pulse rate check. Note down any current physical problems and any medication. In addition note any addictions. The body autobiography and the personal check on oneself are a good precursor to a medical by the GP, which is advisable if you are middle aged or elderly and starting out. Turning up at the GP with written information will save time and will almost certainly mean that you will be taken seriously! Inform the GP what you intend in the way of exercise.

Choose Your Places to Exercise

Green exercise is a great way of getting to really know your locality.

Depending on the activities you choose you will probably need a variety of walking, running or biking routes and places where you can do gym work. If you are able, take some time to walk all the routes you think you will use, and notice any interesting features or peculiarities. Try to locate some possible gym areas – this could be your garden, allotment, a gym trail or delineated exercise area of your local park, or perhaps a steepish hill in a nearby country area. Think 'topophilia' – the love of place – a fascinating area of ecopsychology.

Planning a Programme

If you intend to participate in the green gym, you will need to structure a programme of exercises. It is not my intention here to advise on a schedule – there are plenty of books and websites which will detail the individual movements, many of which will be familiar. Remember that there are five broad areas of exercise one can incorporate into any workout – strength, power, stability, stamina and flexibility – and that it is usually best to work all the major body parts, including the all-important 'core'. In the early stages keep the number of exercises to a low number, maybe five or six. Build up gradually, increase the intensity over time.

Sustenance

Good nutrition is pretty vital; which means a balanced diet avoiding as far as possible processed foods, ready meals, alcohol and sugary drinks. Remember there is a massive food industry which knows perfectly well the textures and tastes that most suit our bodily wants (not needs) and that also knows what makes us addicts. Eat as much fresh food as possible; in the long run it will be much cheaper for you and for society. But don't become a puritan regarding food, just be sensible and treat yourself occasionally.

Rest

Sleeping patterns will almost certainly improve with green exercise and sensible nutrition. It will most likely become a virtuous circle – exercise, food, rest will work together instead of in conflict. There is such a variety of sleep requirements that advice on the number of hours is not really helpful. Try to avoid a flat screen of any kind before you go to bed, and make sure water is the last thing you drink.

Massage/Bodywork

If you are able, try and receive fairly regular massage. There are a wide variety of bodywork therapies which are worth investigating but they can be expensive. If you can afford to treat yourself occasionally, definitely do so. Better still, learn a bodywork therapy yourself – some years ago I did just that, and it taught me a great deal about anatomy and physiology as well as practical massage. Eventually find someone you can swop treatments with.

Doing It

Regularity is essential for good results. Work the green gym and green exercise into your life; it is not always easy to do and self discipline is required. However, you will find that physical self discipline can be learnt like most other things in life; the benefits will follow, sometimes with a lag, but they will come. Those benefits will be physical but they will also be emotional and, if you want, spiritual.

* * *

THE THIRD AWAKENING

Marian Van Eyk McCain

Here I stand, in the sunshine, pegging shirts on the washing line. There is a light breeze blowing. If the weather stays like this, it will be a perfect day for getting this load of laundry dry. My hands are damp and they ache slightly from wringing out all those clothes.

It is early spring, and the woodpeckers are drumming to attract their mates. A thrush is singing. Daffodils nod their bright heads in the flower bed and I can feel the garden coming to life. This week, I shall plant out the first trays of seedlings – kale and cabbage, broccoli and cauliflower, spinach, lettuce, rocket – and firm their roots down into the freshly composted earth.

The sky is bright blue today, with just a few wispy clouds. Somewhere, a few fields away, I can hear a tractor. There is another sound, too, a low thudding, getting closer. I look up to see a helicopter, coming in low over the village. The coastguards probably, patrolling the cliffs. But the sound of its engine, together with the warmth of the spring sunshine on my arms, is prompting a memory. I smile to myself as I think back to that morning – the one where I lost my political virginity.

I had been to many demonstrations in my life, but this was different. Yes, the banners were there, and the microphones and news cameras. There were the usual speeches, the usual cheers and ra-ra-ra. But this time, instead of marching through the city streets, we were in the middle of a field. Hundreds and hundreds of us, from elders to toddlers, all sitting on the grass in the middle of nowhere, in the warm sunshine. Most of the adults were wearing white biohazard suits. A political statement, those – or so I naively assumed when the organizers handed them out. I remember thinking how bizarre it must have looked from the air. When the helicopter pilot gazed down at us, it would have been like looking down on a field full of button mushrooms.

Speeches over, the white mushrooms marched in a long line, through a gate, into another field. Spread out, circled the field. Stood all around the edge with linked arms, still and silent, as previously instructed. A Gilbert & Sullivan chorus line of policemen in reflective vests watched us warily from the eastern side of the field. The helicopter thrummed overhead, endlessly circling. It was a ritual. A tableau. Pointless? Perhaps. But if it was in the papers, that would draw more attention to our campaign. A picture of several hundred people, quietly encircling a field of green plants. Praying, maybe. Willing things to change. "Silly hippies, at it again", some people would remark tomorrow, over breakfast.

But wait – maybe this time it was different. Yes, it was. Suddenly, I knew why we were really here. Any moment now, there would be a signal. Or not so much an overt signal as a movement in group consciousness. And when that moment came, I knew that the circle would break. The crowd would begin surging forward into the field – hesitantly at first and then, gathering courage, with a firmer intent, reaching for the plants and wrenching them from the ground, one by one. The line between peaceful demonstration and law-breaking would have been crossed

Adrenalin surged into my veins. At last, after all these months of reading, writing, stuffing envelopes, signing petitions, attending meetings, making phone calls, I was on the front lines, arm-in-arm with the real warriors. I was about to become a real activist.

The oilseed rape plants, slender but wiry, would resist at first, clinging with their roots to the drying soil. But then they would succumb, as human muscles powered by righteous anger laid waste to the crop. Poor, innocent things. They, like us were being tricked, their natural processes hijacked for the sake of profit. They were being forced to bear, on their bright, yellow pollen, the progeny of rape in more senses than one. So they had to die. To save the purity of our organic crops, these bio-engineered monsters had to be destroyed. I wept for their innocence but I knew that when the signal came I wouldn't hold back. I would destroy. If I got arrested, so be it.

Now I understood what soldiers feel when the drums of battle sound. Suddenly, in that moment, I realised how it would feel to be a martyr, a terrorist, a suicide bomber. I understood how it would feel to put yourself completely on the line and to suffer and die for your cause, your soft body armoured by certainty, all doubt and compassion overridden.

That Was the First Awakening

The second awakening followed a few months later. Once the biotech companies had lost a few of their genetically engineered trial crops to mobs of angry protesters, they strengthened their defences. So when the speeches were done and we marched towards the field – this time, a field of maize – we found our way barred by high, dense hedges, with every gate manned by a dozen police. There would be no more crop-pulling. We faced off, traded insults. A few tried to storm the gates and duly got arrested. The rest glumly circumnavigated the field, thwarted. I felt angry, frustrated, wanting to kill.

But when it was all over and our procession wended its way back, the police walked with us. They turned out to be just ordinary people, dressed in uniform. We chatted as we walked. Most of them didn't particularly favour genetic engineering of food crops either. Probably the helicopter pilot felt the same. They were just working; just following instructions. Suddenly, it all seemed silly. We were acting a charade. All this huffing and puffing and marching and getting arrested felt like a game played by children in a playground. I realised that I didn't want to play the activist game any more.

That Was the Second Awakening

I attended no more protests after that, against genetic engineering or anything else. It felt pointless. 'They' – the powerful corporations, the profiteers, the exploiters and pillagers of Nature, despoilers of the Earth – would always win. What was the point, I wondered, in being an activist? With governments in thrall to corporate capital and millions of people drugged by TV into passivity, what's the use of activism? And what is the point of going to marches and protests when the media – equally in thrall to Big Business – don't even bother reporting on them half the time?

I peg another shirt on the washing line. The breeze fills it and it billows out like a sail in the sunshine, its arms plump with air. The helicopter has gone now and the tractor has stopped. There is only the sound of birdsong. I can smell the tang of the ocean, a few miles away. Oh how I love this life.

Sure, it is hard work, washing the clothes by hand, growing our own vegetables, patrolling for slugs and snails every night with a flashlight. We have to gather wood for kindling, stack logs, chop them. My muscles ache sometimes but it is a good ache. It is the ache of tired satisfaction.

We have no car, no TV, no dishwasher, no microwave. We shop locally, repair, re-use, recycle, bank with an ethical bank, ride the buses and trains, buy second-hand clothes, used books and fair trade coffee beans.

I peg out the last two socks. Then, as I pick up the now empty laundry basket and turn to walk back towards the cottage, a thought comes to me. Is this not activism?

Later, as ponder that thought over a cup of tea, I realise I've just experienced the third awakening.

For I, and all the millions like me who live simply and sustainably, we are the true activists of the 21st century. Rather than fighting fruitless battles to protect the world, we are building a new one instead. A different, alternative world. A sustainable one.

We are building a world powered by sun, wind and water instead of oil. We are building houses of stone and mud and straw bales, studying whatever is around us in our bioregions, rediscovering and rebuilding and reinventing community. We are saving seeds and sowing them, baking bread, spinning, weaving – weaving a world that works for all creatures and one in which humans will finally learn how to live humbly and in sacred synergy with the ecosystem that contains them.

That line of wet washing, that's my true activism. Whenever I walk or ride my bicycle, whenever I tend my garden on hands and knees, eat a home-cooked vegetarian meal or stand at the bus stop on a winter morning feeling feet and fingers growing cold in the wind, am I not putting my body on the line for my beliefs as surely as Joan of Arc?

Maybe we'll succeed in changing the world before it's too late. Maybe we won't. But I know I shall die trying.

When I die, someone might say "She was a lifelong activist, you know." Or maybe they won't. But it doesn't matter. I shall have been one anyway.

*   *   *

PART THREE

WILDNESS

What differentiates deep green living from just living in an eco-friendly sort of way is, as I said in the Introduction, our sense of identification with the planet of whose fabric we are made. We, too, are an intrinsic part of Nature. Our animal bodies, just like the bodies of all other living organisms, are totally made of wild ingredients. Remembering that – and living our lives out of that knowledge – is the essence of deep green living.

WILD GRACE: NATURE AS A SPIRITUAL PATH

Eric Alan

Inside, we are all born for the outside. We breathe the naked air, grow in the light of the raw sun. We spring from the soil as surely as the most tentative grass. Through the astonishing and mysterious grace of the natural ways, we have come to be creatures of awareness as well, capable of wonder, faith and deep feeling. We see the remarkable stretch of the place beyond and below us, and develop spiritual conceptions to make meaning of the vast patterns. For long ages, humanity has applied intuition and knowledge to create paths of spirit, to make sense of the larger universe, and to provide daily guidance for our individual footfalls.

Two thousand years after the founding of the west's dominant religion, spiritual seeking is a resurgent theme. Some who have grown up in a material rather than spiritual culture find themselves sensing an absence, and wishing to return to more calming ground. Others who have pursued traditional faiths find those belief systems now incomplete or inadequate. Many seek to integrate a heightened ecological consciousness with a spiritual one. All of us are challenged by the commingling and collision of different paths, as a global culture increases our exposure to vastly different notions. The result can be a crisis of spirit within the renewed awakening.

There is one spiritual path which contains all others, though; which conflicts with none. It is Nature itself. Nature is the path which fosters the life of all seekers. Nature neither requires nor precludes belief in deity. It includes both creation and evolution, without conflict. It demands no dogmatic rituals, and damns no disbelievers. Nature speaks only silently, offers no absolution, and has hard ways as well as sweet vistas. Yet within its silence and its graceful, tightly woven forms, it offers philosophical and practical answers. In the way that plants, animals and even the elements are and relate to each other, is an almost holographic, complete key to the balance we must find within ourselves and with each other.

We can follow Nature's path through the tiny details of it present in our everyday lives – regardless of where we live and how damaged the natural order may be there. Nature offers a practical spirituality to be integrated into our daily lives as they are, rather than something we must radically alter our usual routines to include. It's a natural mindfulness which sees the whole of the answers to our questions and difficulties in the tiniest details of the living, natural Earth.

What is this spirituality, and how can we apply it daily?

In the answer to this is both a beautiful celebration of the details of the natural world, and a meditation upon living in it. All that's required is our vision. This is a prayer for, and a glimpse of, that vision.

In the Cathedral

At this sweet moment – whichever it is – you're in a cathedral. So am I. Always. Spires of trees may not embrace you as you read this; the soft prayers of stream whispers may be too far beyond walls for hearing. Still we can listen for them, seek them, remember them. We can recognize the clarity that comes from moments in pure wilderness, and learn to hold that clarity inside. We can use our connectedness to recognize that, despite the layers of concrete and pain we have layered over the land, Nature still reaches us. In even the urban settings, which often contain and confine us, there is Nature to be found in every sight, every breath. That breath you're taking right now – which you could live only seconds if disconnected from – is in turn connected to the entire protective atmosphere that embraces the planet. So, too, the sip of water from your glass is connected to every ocean beyond the walls. Even the dust that now settles on your floor is a reminder of connection to Nature, for it's a trace of the elemental ground of home. And in that Nature is clear guidance to our questions. Calm answers to silent prayers.

We are always in the cathedral because we're an integral element of it. Nature is something we are; not just something with which we relate. In the beauty of following Nature as a spiritual path comes an ability to recognize that: to feel Nature's order in ourselves as well as in every surrounding.

For me, it's easier to feel the whole Earth as a divine sanctuary while at the base of a redwood whose patience has lasted a thousand years, than at the end of a traffic jam that seems as if it will last the same. It's easier to flow with the spirit of water at the bedside of a river whose commitment to flow never ceases or tires, than it is at a drinking fountain in the lobby of a sterile city hall.

Yet I've learned that with practice, Nature's vision and reverence can be brought forth via even the smallest, driest urban leaf. It's entirely contained within the fewest lingering drops of dew on back alley windows.

In even the most barriered, forsaken, desperate building, there is still that breath of air to be drawn. And on each breath is a remembrance which is always available: Breathing in, the wind is a part of me. Breathing out, I am a part of the wind. I use it to bring awareness back to the truth of our constant presence in the cathedral. To our integral part in its being.

I find that connecting to Nature's spiritual presence only while in wilderness is akin to only seeking connection with a higher spirit while in church. For those who choose it, that Sunday hour may be vital. It may be restorative and centrally grounding. But it's only one hour of the week. It's the thoughts and deeds of the other hours that put the faith into practice.

It's the ability to see high spirit and beauty everywhere that brings the faithful into the realization of their faith's healing powers. Along other paths, it's one definition of a saint: those who can see beauty in anyone, anywhere, and dare to look that beauty straight in the naked eye; to face the pain that's inevitably within the beauty. I think it no different in looking at Nature. Our own darkest, most violent sides, are a part of Nature too. We are always in the cathedral. We are stones in the cathedral's floor, ourselves.

No Ceilings

One deep reason for seeking a spiritual path is to gain a sense of perspective on the greater order and our place within it. There's limitless comfort in the resulting feeling of belonging. A conscious way of being evolves; a reason emerges for every reverent step, and daily motions become made with certainty. There's also an end to a sense of isolation. Randomness recedes in the face of a clearer view.

So why the proliferation of ceilings which destroy that clearer view? Our warm walls are welcoming and protective at times – they're a strong element of all that we label 'home.' Yet if we dwell too much inside them, we lose a much greater sense of home. We have lost the sky.

Our little constructions of plaster, wood and steel do exactly what they're designed to do: contain us. And sometimes that's nice. In winter, it's essential. Yet when all of Nature is the cathedral, being contained under ceilings is like sitting under a cardboard box in church. All the spacious sights, sounds and other sensuous connections are muffled, even suffocated. All the realizations that they bring are dulled as well. There's a sadness in ceilings that the vigilant can't deny.

Light, illumination, is what we often say we're seeking when staring at questions and challenges. Yet, out from under those restrictive ceilings, it's the dark night sky which often allows the best soothing return of perspective. In that sky and beyond it, almost all of the cathedral rests.

It extends beyond the borders of perception, even aided with the most miraculous telescopes. But we need no technological aid to regain perspective. We need no electricity. In fact, the perspective of the stars is best gathered without it. With no electric lights in the vicinity, a simple upward glance returns us to a clear view of our almost invisible celestial place.

The purity of a wilderness sky, though, is rare for any of us to be able to reach with regularity. The wilderness has been driven out of our homes, and with it has gone the wild grace it placed in our hearts alongside the hard danger. We have to reach for what slivers of sky are available to us, and learn to be grateful that with a practiced eye, an open window and one star will do, for clear vision and remembrance.

Each star makes its steady, persistent statement of scale and presence regardless of the attention of any viewers. That kind of persistence and steadiness has been one of the greatest lessons for me, has provided one of the best role models, in pursuing my path of expression. The stars inspire me to continue being my true self as best as I can, regardless of my distance from the crowd, or my invisibility within it. The stars teach me to continue speaking my quiet truth even if there seem to be no listeners. Words, like starlight, can take far longer than their source's life to reach their destination.

There are those who find our infinitesimal size frightening – especially compared to the distance between even the most neighbourly stars. Some cannot look at the stars for fear of disappearing alongside. But our smallness doesn't make us insignificant. In fact the vast black stretches where no life dwells make this planet's exception that much more sacred; our own life within its weave is that much more precious.

In our own near disappearance is also the largest personal comfort. There's infinite room to breathe deeply, mindfully. In that space of breathing under the stars, your own airy rhythm can easily contain whatever ails you.

Explore tonight: take the largest problem you currently have with you, to whatever sliver of sky you have available. One window and one star will do if they have to. Focus on that star and breathe, and remember patience; for remember how long the light from that star has taken to reach you. Give it respect, and give it attention; for that particular starlight, after its journey of ages, will have traveled for naught if you ignore it. It will never return. Its tone is as pure as that of a bell – harmonize with it. Sing to it and breathe. And again compare yourself and that problem to the distance. If you can still remember that problem by now.

You are far larger than your problem; and you too have noticed how you vanish against that star. No matter if the problem is one of love, family, friendship, career, health, trauma, disconnection from spirit ... It, even more than you, fades into nothing in face of the stars. Even our planetary tug-of-wars and environmental screams cannot cross the smallest black gulf to trouble our closest neighbors. Our problems are tiny, remote, and yet we are centered exactly on the point of the only living sphere for a great stretch of space. A freedom from ceilings, and we immediately remember.

No Floors

On occasion, just for a moment, I catch a glimpse of the truth of the universe. It's not an intellectual grasping of some serious large Truth; it's not a mind understanding at all. It's just a fleeting, wordless awareness in the heart: it's a pure sensation of grasping the absolute, wondrous, unknowable enormity of all that exists beyond our tiny sphere of perception. It instills an awe that washes all tension and thought from my soul. All voices are silenced inside. Only the breath remains.

That silence only lasts for an instant, before the tides of chattering verbiage veil my awareness once more. But those instants are enough to instill lasting memory, and memory of that truth helps bring the awareness forward again.

The silence of the awe was most reachable at first for me through the grace of the night sky. It was only after enough brief openings to the truth of the endless natural wonder that I began to sense that the same cleansing awe, the purifying silence and refreshment of the soul, could be found as easily through the miracle of the minuscule as well as the extensive. The endlessness that pervades the sky also informs the distance that separates us from – and connects us to – the unknowably small.

At each level between our own existence and that of the smallest particle, an entirely distinct world exists, radically different but not separate from our own.

It was glass that began to show this to me most clearly. More clearly than if the glass was not there at all. A certain kind of glass; a focused glass through which focused vision developed. The lenses of my camera allowed me to enter the Earth at a level other than my own. That level wordlessly showed me what it was to feel the truth of small color. How does the bold red of a single blooming petal feel to the senses, when it's large enough to fill the whole vision? How does it feel to be the insect absorbed in the world of crawling across that petal?

I learned I could cross huge vistas by disappearing into the tiny. Suddenly I knew that there are no floors, ultimately, any more than there are ceilings. There is no ground so solid as to be impermeable to vision. This changed everything.

In the miniature worlds at my feet, now, with or without lenses, I can see realities as removed from our own as that of unknown creatures orbiting distant stars. The differing lives and realities are at the end of our skin on all sides, within a place small enough to require great sensitivity to see, smell and taste. Even more than that: the endless levels are inside of us too – it's obvious and yet continually forgotten. Inside, lives of blood cells and bacteria and other life know our bodies as the universe, as surely as we in turn only know the belly of a larger universe that we cannot conceive beyond. It too, may be only one body of unknowable billions.

Peering into the endlessness of small details – countless levels of which exist beyond even the reach of the best assistive lens – restores perspective as much as another comforting disappearance under the stars. Just sitting, closely watching the tiny details at your feet, is a practice that can bring release as well as perspective. It is indeed a practice, just as yoga and meditation are practices; and in fact yoga and meditation have much to do with the perspective of the details and the stars. Every yoga pose asks for a counterpose for balance: perspective asks the same. A view of the enormous sky asks for a view of a single inch of soil at our feet. Only with both is there completeness, and only with bringing a meditative, still eye to both is there depth.

While disappearance into a field of untouchable stars returns a comforting smallness, and gives a soft dark blanket to be deeply enfolded in, disappearance into the tiny returns an equally valid sense of our great effect on the small elements of the world – elements which provide the basis of our lives. Every footstep can respect or crush a thousand tiny lives; each breath inhales and expels more life than we can measure.

The spiritual path which preaches avoidance of all harm to any individual creature, while noble in its intention and result, is not what Nature teaches by example. Instead it teaches the necessary loss of individuals in favor of the greater balance. In its insistence on struggle, Nature teaches the central role of pain as well as peace in the higher harmony. It's a hard spirituality, in that sense. It offers no promise of a sweet by-and-by; not even a certainty of a soft present – although it does not preclude either.

What it offers instead is a staggering depth of real beauty in each present moment. It offers an unspoken proof of the remarkable possibilities of higher harmony between millions of species – of collaboration within the struggle to produce an astonishing weave of graceful life – all with no effort more than instinct required. It offers the knowledge to the observant that beauty exists on so many levels that we can only begin to imagine how beautiful our own world is, let alone the totality of the exquisite universe it's nestled in, and whatever may lie beyond.

In recognizing our power over the tiny lives we often don't even perceive, Nature grants us an opportunity to develop respect and consideration in every footstep. It also offers an awareness of our individual strength. Through our relation to the small details, we can come to know that there is great cause and effect in every motion. To know that despite the enormity of the universe, we have an enormity of our own. This appears true for each creature within the great chain of sizes that we can perceive.

We are therefore, in that regard, exactly equal to the creatures and living systems above and below us in that chain of size. So do we not have equal responsibility to be humble before that order? To participate in it and care for it as it needs? And since instinct provides all the care necessary for the balanced evolution, is it not true that every step away from instinct and into intellect has led us away from balance and into 'civilization'? True civilization and progress would mean an evolution within Nature's balanced order, and not one which transiently arranges human comfort at the expense of all else.

To return to the beauty of floorless details can return a soul in an instant to a more balanced place of the heart. I find that a view of an insect on a leaf, for instance – seen without the temptation to analyze, classify, capture or otherwise disturb – can return me to that inner balanced view without effort or words. That's a remarkable discovery: that despite the key elements of struggle within Nature's path, it's an absence of struggle that returns the heart to balance.

That place of balance is a place of pure sensation. A place of simultaneously knowing our enormity, our tininess, our equality, our strength and vulnerability. It's a calming silence we were born to know.

*　*　*

The above is excerpted, by permission, from Eric Alan's book of photography and writing entitled *Wild Grace: Nature as a Spiritual Path* (White Cloud Press 2003.) As well as a photographer, author and blogger, Eric is the music, arts and culture host for National Public Radio affiliate KLCC in Eugene, Oregon. He lives in Cottage Grove, Oregon, USA.

REWILDING MYSELF
Rachel Corby

I am a true believer that the changes you wish to see in the world you must first initiate within yourself.

There has been a lot of talk in recent times of rewilding landscapes, of returning species once prevalent but absent for in some cases extended periods of time back to their rightful area, in essence bringing them home. It has been proved in the great wild open spaces of America that such actions have a positive feedback on the environment. That reintroducing top predators, for example, changes the feeding habits of grazers as they need to remain more undercover. This allows certain plant species to grow to maturity or to recolonise. As they do so, birds, insects, small mammals and plant species that thrive alongside those plants also return. A great experiment with very positive results. However there is something missing from this formula for me. Human activity contributed to, or in many cases was entirely responsible for, the environmental degradation of those areas and the removal of certain species in the first place. So any attempt to restock with animals and rebuild the ecological interactions of such sites, unless in protected areas such as National Parks, will surely come up against the same issues that originally led to the removal of those species in the first place. Protected areas aside, we cannot rewild our nature areas successfully without first adjusting our individual attitudes and personal relationship with the wild.

Humanity needs rebalancing, just as areas of land do. We should remember that we were born to this planet as wild creatures. Our domestication, however, began almost immediately as we emerged into sanitised hospital conditions and modern life. Yet at our core each and every one of us remains wild.

My personal journey has been rather typical. Cut off from Nature shortly after birth, my later teenage years were spent in the midst of an environmental crisis. Initially depletion of the ozone layer and acid rain while climate change, species extinctions, deforestation and pollution continue to be of great concern. As a teenager it broke my heart every day. I felt like an alien that had been dropped into an uncaring synthetic world. It made me sick; I was depressed, angry, disaffected and lonely.

My experience was not unique. A World Health Organisation report from 2014, "Health for the World's Adolescents", concluded that the single largest cause of illness in teenagers worldwide is depression, with suicide being the third largest cause of death. Shocking statistics. Teenagers are not the only ones suffering of course, and lack of Nature in our lives and the environmental crisis are not the only reasons behind such statistics, but they most certainly contribute.

Almost by accident, my first step toward wholeness was to notice where I felt most well, most vibrant and alive. It is perhaps no surprise that it was in areas of wild Nature: a walk in the woods, a swim in a lake, a walk on the beach; we have all felt it, felt our bodies sing and our spirits soar in such places. My next step was to figure out how to bring that home, how to, as much as possible, remain connected to such vital and real sensations and feelings.

A major breakthrough came when I rediscovered the livingness of the world, the realisation that I am connected to all life and that everything is alive! I began to recognise plants and stones, rivers, the soil as living entities with personalities, with spirit, with feeling. As soon as I began to acknowledge that, everything changed. I now notice other beings, I talk to them; it has become an essential part of my moment to moment existence.

I still move things aside when needs be, but I ask them and

communicate with them, no longer stuff in the way but a tree branch pulsating with life, a stone full of wisdom and stories to tell. I noticed that objects I had previously considered inanimate have feelings to them. That a hand carved wooden spoon feels so much more alive than a factory moulded plastic one. I removed paint from everything in my house that is made of wood – skirting boards, floor boards, doors – as I became aware of the presence of the ancient soul who grew that wood as their body. Now as I touch the wood I offer it love and gratitude and I remember my relative, the tree, who was sacrificed so that I could live in this way, in this house.

It began slowly for me, rewilding, reintroducing wild elements into my life, but it has brought the balance and the joy back, just as it has done in the areas of America where top predators have been reintroduced.

It has pervaded all areas of my life. Just as the sun's warmth on my skin and the breeze ruffling my hair feeds me, I have become so aware of what I put inside my body and how that makes me feel. I love to grow food and medicine plants, I love to forage. At all stages of the process from planting the seed to gathering the fruit I constantly communicate. I talk, I listen, I ask, I thank. And so what ends up on my plate and in my belly has so much more life force than produce that has been transported around the planet, that has been processed, even local produce purchased at the farmers market. There is something more real and more alive when my relationship with that food is strong and has been consciously nurtured. What I then feed myself with, what becomes the cells of my body, my blood, my flesh, are my relatives, my children, my lovers. I know that one day, when I return to dust, when my flesh becomes earth once more, I will feed back to the soil the plants I have held in my cells all this time and the cycle will roll on.

I have learnt to listen to and communicate with my body. To tune in to my senses, to use them fully. There appears to be little more grounding and energising than taking a moment to sit outside with awareness. When I have spent too long inside working at the computer I like to do just that. I choose a patch and sit on the ground, eyes closed. Then I listen. I listen to all the sounds; the different birds and insect buzzes, the rustling in the undergrowth and between the leaves high up in the canopy. Then I turn my attention to what my skin can tell me, sticky grass or dusty soil, scratchy twigs and smooth pebbles. Then I look in great detail, face low to the ground. How many different plants in that tiny space the different shades of green and brown, the pinks and yellows. The insects and the plants. Then I smell. The smell on the breeze, the different aroma each bloom and leaf offers up. Once I have asked, I taste. A little nibble of this and that. It is amazing the array of flavours the plants covering a tiny patch of ground contain; bitter, sweet, fresh, sour. As I work through each sense I understand more of the complexity and variety that life offers, and I feel more a part of it. Sinking into the feelings I meld with the earth as it cradles my form, I feel myself becoming Nature once more and my wildness grows.

Rewilding for me is that simple. For once one's own wildness is acknowledged, and relatives are recognised all around, communications open up and everything changes. I can no longer live the way I once did, half asleep, missing multiple interactions every hour, thinking I am alone when I am surrounded by life, life that is part of myself. I will never again forget that I am Nature, wild Nature. For the Nature 'out there', on the mountain hillsides of Wales or even in our own back gardens, to be healthy and to thrive, the nature inside must be so too. At the most basic and fundamental level there is no separation.

For the planet to be strong, wildness must thrive and for that it is my belief that we need more than a token effort to reintroduce wild animals somewhere at the fringes of our reach. If each person were to start acknowledging all beings as alive, as relatives. If each person were to consider how each object in their home, and the very fabric of their house feels. If each person were to consider everything they eat – what it is made of, where it came from, how it makes them feel once consumed. And if each person were to bask in Nature whenever they get the chance whether in an urban park during lunch hour or a rugged coastline while on holiday. Just imagine how different life for all of us could be.

My wish for humanity is that each person rediscovers their personal wildness, rediscovers how good, how energising and revitalising it feels to feed that wildness; that is my dream. I have learned that dreams remain dreams unless you action them, unless you do something positive to move towards them every day. And so I nurture my personal wildness, I eat wild and raw, I walk barefoot on lush grass, I swim naked in wild water, I talk to my plants. As I do so I feel wilder, stronger, more alive and more awake and slowly but surely I have noticed that the environment I am immersed within is responding, it too is becoming wilder and stronger. Slowly, slowly the dream becomes real.

*   *   *

Rachel is a plant whisperer, Nature dreamer, biophile. She is the author of three books: *Rewild Yourself: Becoming Nature* **(CreateSpace, 2015) being the most recent. Rachel is a rewilding coach and runs workshops, retreats and 1-2-1 sessions on plant consciousness and Sacred Plant Medicine. She also leads a Sacred Ecology apprenticeship. www.gatewaystoeden.com.**

PART FOUR

RELATIONSHIP

Deep green living means, above all, living in a way that acknowledges our total embeddedness in the web of life and our complete interdependence with all the other beings who make up our world. One of the biggest barriers to living this way is that we have all been inculcated with the idea that we humans are somehow separate from the rest of Nature, rather than an intrinsic part of it. In our ignorance and arrogance we have set ourselves apart, believing not only that we are more intelligent than any other animals but that we have this special thing we call consciousness that other animals don't. As the first essay reminds us, influential thinkers of an earlier century even believed that our human role was to 'conquer' Nature.

We now know, of course, how ignorant, arrogant and downright damaging those ideas were. Sadly, the remnants still linger. Humanity still tends to see the Earth as merely a playground and a larder for humans and its other creatures as 'things.' However, modern research is showing what the shamans have always known, which is that all beings have consciousness in some degree or other and that there are various types of intelligence, some of which are possessed in even greater quantities in many of our fellow beings than they are in us.

As we come to realize, through this chapter's fascinating glimpse into the lives of the elephants of Namibia, we are not the only animals who think and plan, solve problems, suffer stress, help and rescue those in trouble, mourn our dead and cherish our loved ones. Yes, we have uniquely human ways of doing all these things, but maybe we should call that culture, not Nature. It is within our differing cultures – our habits and ways of being as the type of creatures that we are – where the differences lie. In the depths of Nature is where we find our sameness.

Many of us are fascinated by other human cultures and enjoy learning about them. And when we can transcend political and ideological differences and have a sense of ourselves as being part of the one vast tribe of humankind, we are able to respect and honour those other human cultures and see them as different but equal. In exactly the same way, when we have a deep sense of ourselves as just another different but equal part of Nature –part of the tribe of All Earth – I believe that we find ourselves not only wanting to learn more about the cultures of the other life forms around us but feeling a deep sense of honour and respect towards them. With that attitude, any meeting between our life and theirs can become a sacred encounter. Later in this chapter, is the brief description of one such simple moment in the writer's own backyard. Many of us have had such an experience and treasured it. Relationship is precious and it is vital. Not only relationship with our own kind, but with all the other life forms who, along with us, make up the fabric of Earth.

NATURE – WHO WILL CONQUER IT?

Nigel Lees

"I am the dreadful menace the one whose will is done, the haunting chill upon your neck….". This ponderous quote introduced the BBC's coverage of the 2014 Sochi Winter Olympics. The trailer ends with the line: Nature – who will conquer it? Although Nature has been seen in some cultures as sacred and to be treated with reverence, awe and wonder, the current myth in our mainstream globalized culture – now reinforced by an increase in floods and natural disasters worldwide, seems to be that Nature, is something to fight against. There are two prevailing views on this. One view, typified by David Abram and reflected in his book *The Spell of the Sensuous*, describes how some indigenous cultures had and still have a connection to the animistic spirit in Nature; that Nature is alive and numinous.

The counter view illustrated by Yuval Noah Harari in his book *Sapiens*, shows that wherever Homo Sapiens migrated to, extinction of megafauna soon followed. Of course harsh climatic changes may well have had a major affect as well but early humans, he suggests, were responsible for most of the extinctions.

The humans who migrated to Australia about 60,000 years ago and who may have helped kill off the megafauna, eventually developed into a culture that gave us the `Dreamtime' as well as a way of living in harmony with Nature. Is this happening with our dominant culture today? Let us hope that we can learn much faster than the first Australians to live with and not against Nature, as we do not have thousands of years left to get it right.

We are the only species (that we know of) with the super power of imagination, which along with curiosity, created civilisations, the arts, science and technology. In this article I'd like to explore how we have tried to exceed and tame Nature and examine ways in which cooperation is the best way forward, by choosing examples that are not immediately obvious.

The Picturesque Earth?

Seeing is important and tells us a lot about how we view Nature. Yuri Gagarin, the first man in space, said before lift off: "To be the first to enter the cosmos, to engage, single-handed, in an unprecedented duel with Nature – could one dream of anything more?" However, on seeing the Earth for the first time from orbit he remarked :"…Mankind, let us preserve and increase this beauty, and not destroy it". The space race may have been a testosterone fuelled Olympian competition but it led astronaut Eugene Cernan, the last man to walk on the moon, to comment: "We went to explore the moon and, in fact, discovered the earth". The most famous photograph from space is Earthrise taken on December 24th 1968. We see for the very first time how fragile and alone this blue home of ours is. Contrast this stark, uncompromising but beautiful photograph with the view from Earth over 180 years ago. The Rev William Gilpin, one of the leading lights of the picturesque, which was a late 18th century movement concerned with aesthetic qualities in the landscape, held that Nature could be improved upon in capturing the perfect picture. Gilpin wrote in 1782: "Nature is always great in design. She is an admirable colourist also; and harmonizes tints with infinite variety and beauty: but she is seldom so correct in composition, as to produce a harmonious whole."

Though perhaps an unfashionable term now, the picturesque was a major influence on the sculptured landscape and the tourist industry, where the whole of Nature can be caged in a digital image. What a lovely view.

Pairidaeza

The garden, like much of our landscape in the UK, is a totally man-made creation. Gardens were first developed about 3,000 years ago in the Middle East where they were enclosed in order to separate them (and by implication the home) from the chaos and wildness that abounds in Nature. The garden became a place of civilisation where the powerful could create elaborate displays of man's authority over Nature. The Persian name for these enclosures was pairidaeza from which we get the English world paradise; the garden came to represent an earthly paradise, a haven for the spirit. Though gardens can be very beautiful:

> *A garden is a symbol of man's arrogance, perverting nature to human ends.*
>
> – Tim Smit, in *The Lost Gardens of Heligan.*

Tim Smit's quote may seem harsh, but he does go on to say "…and humans are part of nature…a perverse dilemma!" Dilemma indeed, as controlling Nature and people is what humans have done best. Gardening may seem to be one of the ways in which we happily show that we are in charge. Only we are not. Without the use of expensive chemicals many of us feel that we cannot `control' – weeds or pests or increase soil fertility. The garden thus becomes a `battle ground', `Nature red in tooth and claw' and even an `evolutionary arms race'.

Animal Farm

Displaying animals in a menagerie goes back thousands of years. Powerful rulers wanted to demonstrate their power over other species as well. These enclosures of wild animals were replicated throughout the centuries until they became entertainment in circuses and zoos. Now zoos are re-branded as environmental and conservation organisations. A Radio 4 programme on Animal Architecture 30th July 2014 raised many of these issues. Zoos are part of the way humans have of classifying the natural world. Put everything in a cage: arboretums for trees; aquariums for sea creatures; botanical gardens for plants; zoos for animals; and perhaps offices for humans. What attracts us to wild animals is their wildness, their `otherness', so we imprison them in cages, keeping them under our control. This desire leads us to create a state for the animals where they can no longer exhibit the wildness for which we loved and feared them in the first place.

Back to the Frontier: From Conquering to Cooperation

For most of existence humans had to be close to Nature; notice the signs in the sky, the weather, movement of water and behaviour of birds and animals. If they didn't they would not survive. It is no wonder that humans felt a spirit move throughout their world. The mountains were alive and humans came to learn to `think like a mountain'. For much of the last 70,000 years the actions of humans, though considerable in parts, have been minimal taken overall. However during the last 500 years the effect of science, technology, lifestyle and population are no longer local but global. This is a familiar story the end result of which is the invention of consumerism and a bored, compliant, envious consumer dominating Nature by proxy.

Perhaps what is less well known is the story of how we are trying to change the culture from working against Nature to learning to work with her. It is less well known because we are still making it up as we go along. Thomas Berry, in his book *The Great Work* said, "Because the exaltation of the human and the subjugation of the

123

natural world have been so excessive, we need to understand how the human community and the living forms of the Earth might now become a life-giving presence to each other." That's a good place to start.

The Power of Flower

We spoke of the garden as a `battle ground' where we try to control the natural order. However, in doing so, we could be interfering with the extraordinary relationship between flower and pollinator. This is a beautiful example of mutual co-operation. The flowering plant gets to reproduce while the pollinator gets a tasty treat and its survival. In turn we get much of the food on our table. If we want to garden in a wildlife-friendly way, one of the fundamental principles is that the garden is a place of balance. Nature is the original `selfish co-operator'. This partnership between flower and insect has been around for millions of years. Pollination is not done for the benefit of humans; it is a green contract between plant and pollinator. We love our bumblebees, honey bees and butterflies, but are we likely to extend the same largesse to the gooseberry sawfly? If we don't then perhaps we should. We benefit from this relationship with Nature only as long as we maintain a balance and do not over exploit (or destroy) the ecosystem. We are now beginning to understand how important the gardener is in supporting biodiversity by sustaining and creating habitat.

Re-wilding Gaia

Over 70 years ago there were no wolves left in Yellowstone National Park in the US. Gradually the elk population increased which started having a negative effect on the ecology of the park. Tree species declined and river banks became badly eroded. The reason for this was thought to be the loss of the top predator – the wolf. George Monbiot describes this story in his TED lecture

2013 For more wonder, re-wild the world. In 1995 the wolf was re-introduced. Though the wolves did kill significant numbers of elks their main affect was to alter elk behaviour. Over years, the biodiversity recovered. Monbiot believes that re-wilding is a good example of Gaia Theory in action; that the Earth is a self regulating organism. Gaia is the name of the scientific theory uncovered by James Lovelock and Lynn Margulis. Lovelock describes Gaia as a "whole system of animate and inanimate parts" whose very life forms (all plants, animals, microorganisms) help to regulate and sustain life within acceptable limits. Though re-wilding may not be appropriate everywhere, it has become a metaphor for working with Nature.

Networks

Though the 19th and especially 20th centuries are thought to have brought about the greatest human destruction of Earth systems in the past few thousand years, it has also brought about an awakening of consciousness. One of the great movements today is in the meeting of our evolutionary journey with spirit. The writings and wisdom of people like Pierre Teilhard de Chardin, Thomas Berry, Brian Swimme and conservationists such as John Muir and Aldo Leopold have helped to inspire thousands of networks all over the world to develop an environmental movement and a spirituality in tune with Nature and not against her.

Rachel Carson's *Silent Spring* in 1962 was an environmental wake up call for a generation. Another milestone came in 1987 with the World Commission on Environmental Development, which defined `sustainability' as: "development that meets the needs of the present without compromising the ability of future generations to meet their own needs". Don't cut down more trees in the forest than you can grow.

Nature – Let's Work with Her

I started this brief enquiry into our relationship with Nature as a response to the BBC's strapline for the Winter Olympics. I see all around me examples that implies that this view on Nature is still very current. Yet despite all this we are the first civilisation to be consciously aware of our effect on the natural world and do something about it. That at least must give us hope.

Our journey is not just a scientific one; it is a spiritual one, a cultural one, an artistic and creative one. We need to remember that we share the Earth with a multitude of other species and that they have rights too. The desire to conquer, control and condition Nature has to be sublimated into a desire to co-operate and show compassion to everything around us. The true 'frontier' of our evolutionary progress is learning to regard Nature in terms of co-operation and balance. We are just beginning to become conscious of the idea that co-operation in Nature, and in society, is as vital as competition. Balance is the key. Good balance is as important in caring for the Earth as it is when you're on skis in those Winter Olympics.

* * *

Nigel Lees was a scientific librarian for 20 years and is now an Interfaith Minister searching for spirit in the garden and beyond. He lives in Chepstow, Wales.

CHANCE ENCOUNTER

Peter Quince

This summer has seen so many warm, sunny days and pure blue skies, and my garden seems to have collared most of them. I do not wish to be selfish – I am willing to share the sun with anyone – but I kind of regard that first hour of the day, when the slant-rays of the ascending sun kiss my garden and reflect its surfaces like a many-faceted diamond, as my own. Is that selfish? Not really. The sun blesses us all and what's more links us intimately wherever we happen to be in the world.

Let me tell you about one particular morning in July, very early, just after first light. I am in the habit of going through the t'ai chi form first thing and very often feel obliged to do so indoors in winter, or when the weather's too wet or too chilly. This summer, drawn by unusual warmth and crystalline light out in the dawn-breaking garden, I very often ventured down to an expanse of lawn between my greenhouse and a high hedge, a place of particular resonance.

One almost cloudless and utterly still morning, before six o'clock, I stood facing east with closed eyes. Already the bright sun gave an aura to the wigwam of beans and reflected off the greenhouse glass and, most pleasantly, warmed my face. I stood in silent meditation. The only sound was birdsong and the sound of the sea in my ears. It felt both vital and mysterious and, for a fleeting moment, I wished others to come and experience the joy that I felt, a sense of the numinous, a profound connectivity

But I was equally happy with a sort of solitude which, paradoxically, convinced me that I was far from alone. I was removed from human company but not from Nature.

It is a great wonder to stand in the midst of life, comprising a miniscule fragment, and sense the Earth turning.

Standing barefoot on the lawn, slowly opening my eyes, catching sight of the sun's rays piercing great cumulus clouds which had bubbled up from nowhere, I felt what I can only describe as an intense groundedness and a heightened sensitivity.

When I had completed the t'ai chi form I moved very slowly, with great deliberation, around familiar nooks of the garden, aware of far more than I am normally, as a muck-and-mulch gardener, aware of.

I studied spiders' webs which reflected sunlight through clinging moisture; I observed with unusual clarity the fascinating features of a snail and the rhythms of its tiny 'antennae'; I gazed long at resting butterflies, their wings semi-transparent like finest gossamer; and little shimmering spirals of gnats rising and falling. In the near silence all seemed surpassingly beautiful, chaotic and yet ordered. It felt like a homecoming. Finally I stood still under the benediction of the sun, closed my eyes once more, insatiable, drinking in the world through my senses.

When I opened my eyes at long last, something appeared peripherally in my vision. I turned my head with practised slowness. A fox stood staring up at me; she was no more than six feet away.

We shared a moment's silence, a rare connection, eye contact. When she walked away, unhurried, behind a shed, I felt the hairs prickle on my neck. I felt both privileged and transformed. The image of that vixen and what the chance meeting meant remains with me today.

*   *   *

SILENT THUNDER
GENTLE MINDS

Eleanor O'Hanlon

April 2015. Damaraland. North-West Namibia

The winter rains came late to Northern Namibia this year, soaking the dry sand rivers that cross the desert and springing clusters of yellow flowers from the red-brown soil. The flowers are bright as saffron in the afternoon sun, and their scent is as rich and sensual as jasmine oil on sun-warmed skin.

A lone elephant, a male, is feeding among the flowers. He delicately bunches, plucks and lifts them with his trunk tip, then taps – once, twice – against a tusk to shake the soil from the stems, before tucking them in his mouth. Great ears fan slowly back and forth, and the rhythm of his movements – plucking, tapping, lifting – is unhurried, as steady as slow waves breaking on a shore, and as calming.

Behind him, the glowing plain of yellow flowers and long grasses, tufted with silver at the tips, is broken by kopjes, rough pyramids of russet-coloured boulders. The Brandberg – Namibia's great 'fiery mountain' – rises along the horizon, a purple mass of granite and feldspar some 2,500 metres tall, which first pierced the crust of this oldest of all deserts over 125 million years ago.

At intervals the elephant scoops up a trunkful of red soil and casts it high over head and shoulders to coat his skin with earth as protection against the sun. He's a mature male, rising massively at the shoulders; his temporal glands are streaming down his cheeks, indicating that he is entering musth, the heightened sexual state in male elephants. But his body posture remains relaxed and his fringed brown eyes are calm.

He knows and trusts our vehicle which belongs to EHRA (Elephant Human Relations Aid) a small organisation dedicated to the protection of Namibia's desert elephants. He would have recognised the engine sound from a distance, for, like all elephants, he has special sensors in the soles of his feet that pick up vibrations travelling through the Earth's crust. His name is Voortrekker, which means 'the pioneer' or 'the one who shows the way' and I have learned a little of his story. Back in the mid-1990s Voortrekker appeared alone along the Huab and Ugab dry river beds. There were no elephants in the area at the time. The poaching which had raged across much of Africa throughout the 1980s, along with competition with farmers for water, had eliminated them all.

Nobody knows where Voortrekker came from originally. He may have walked several hundred miles from further North across the arid scrublands and waterless gravel plains. He stayed around the dry river beds for a while, checking for underground water sources that could be released through digging. He tried the pods and leaves of the ana trees and the aromatic commifora trees, with their ample water stores in the trunk. Then he left, and when he returned, some time later, he was accompanied by a small group of family and friends.

These elephants and their descendants have inhabited this part of Damaraland ever since. Although they belong to the same species as the African savannah elephant, *Loxodonta africana*, Namibia's desert elephants have developed a special culture, based on their experience of the arid conditions. They drink much less frequently than savannah elephants, and they must dig to bring underground water to the surface. In the dry seasons, they walk for long distances to find water, and the difficulties of desert life mean that they reproduce slowly.

Voortrekker remains the senior male in this area, the desert patriarch, and the probable father of most of the youngsters that have since been born. Elephant females prefer experience and maturity in their mates, and young males are rarely accorded this privilege before their mid-thirties. I don't know how old Voortrekker is now – maybe between fifty and sixty-five years of age. He is in that long period of elephant maturity, which spans the arrival of their sixth and final set of molars around the age of thirty, to the time when these last teeth wear down to the gums, without replacements, and Voortrekker, like all his race, will no longer be able to feed himself and will surely know that death approaches.

Voortrekker drapes his trunk with a certain casual elegance across one tusk, and turns towards the jeep. For the first time I see his entire extraordinary face, framed by the great ears that fan gently, opening wide like wings – the domed skull dusted with red, the forehead's bony arch, dipping to soft hollows at both temples above his eyes, his majestic, spreading tusks and muscled trunk.

Elephants have an innate power and presence that you immediately recognize. Beyond their physical grandeur, and the epic scale of their lives, you sense a depth of being that commands your silence and attention. Consider, for a moment, the courage and insight that Voortrekker has shown in his life. Think of his ability to guide others and inspire them with trust and confidence. The wisdom that is born from long, considered experience, the ability to reflect, evaluate circumstances, make the right choices for the good of all, and communicate clearly, even under pressure – these are qualities which transcend the limits the science of animal behaviour placed on animal awareness and cognition.

Over the last twenty-five years, a number of outstanding field researchers have shattered those limits. The boundary between human, and non-human awareness has begun to dissolve into renewed recognition of relationship, and our continuity of being with all life.

The long-term studies into elephant lives led by Joyce Poole, Cynthia Moss, Dame Daphne Sheldrick, Katie Payne, Iain Douglas-Hamilton and others are especially illuminating. They reveal elephants as individuals, with rich inner lives, and a great capacity for relationship, empathy, caring and cooperation. These qualities of connectedness are the ones which are most valued and cherished in elephant communities. Don't they sound familiar? They're exactly the qualities that we humans need as well.

"When I'm out here in the desert, with these elephants, I feel everything is ok. There is peace. I forget all the rubbish that is happening in the world" EHRA leader Chris says as we camp that evening by a kopje, beneath red-ochre boulders lit and burning in the sunset. We spread a tarpaulin on the ground and sleep in the open, under the brilliant span of stars, the spiral band of the galaxy, arching across the southern sky. Reluctant to close my eyes on such matchless splendour, I gaze up at the stars in the Southern Cross, and remember the other elephants we encountered.

We came upon one family resting under the mopane trees – four female adults, each with a youngster at her side, ranging from a few months to a few years of age. They stood bunched together in the shade, slowly swishing ears and tails against the heat and swarms of mopane bees. This is the G6 group, EHRA leader Chris says, and he points out Bellatrix, the matriarch, standing at the edge. Because adult males and females live separately, female relatives remain together as a family and raise their young together. Elephants develop slowly through childhood and adolescence, and they learn by example within these constant, loving relationships, for, like us, elephants do most of their cognitive and emotional development after birth.

The matriarch, usually the oldest, leads the family, and makes the decisions on which their well-being depends. Where shall we go to find water today? Will there be enough time to rest and shelter on the way? Will the youngest baby struggle to keep up? Experience matters, and so does the ability to consider the situation, and make choices for the good of all. Not all elephants make such confident leaders. In Amboseli, in Kenya, Joyce Poole has seen family groups join and follow one that is being led by a particularly resourceful female guide.

After we had watched them in silence for a while, a subtle signal to relax must have passed from the matriarch Bellatrix to the others because one by one the youngsters lay down and went peacefully to sleep. The four mothers watched over them, tossing protective trunkfuls of dust to shield sensitive skins from the sun.

Those moments in the breathing quiet of the afternoon, when the devoted mothers opened their trust and allowed their vulnerable babies to relax completely and go to sleep in our presence were intensely moving. The last time I saw wild elephants was in Zambia's Luangwa Valley, in 1989 at the height of the last poaching crisis. At the sound of our engine, that group had bunched together in defensive formation, adults ringing the young and vulnerable with their bodies.

But here we have been able to share peace. I sensed the rootedness of their being, their ancient belonging on the Earth. In their presence, I too returned to peace, in the unity of being.

But that peace is fragile: water is a precious resource in Damaraland and the desert elephants compete with farmers by drinking from the wells they use to water their cattle and goats. EHRA works to protect the elephants by minimizing the conflict: our small group of volunteers has spent the last week building elephant-proof walls around one farmer's windmill well, which the elephants had damaged when they drank. Mixing concrete, setting large stones in place, in desert heat, with no water for washing at the end of the day was hard work, and one of the most satisfying things I have ever done. For now, at least, these elephants live in peace. But without EHRA's dedication, they might not be here at all.

The next day is pure magic. We meet all the local families – the G6 again, the Ugab family, the Mama Africa group – 33 elephants, with lively babies, curious young adults, elders, males and females, gathering in the same area. Elephants live in nested social networks, from intimate small families to extended families, all the way to their wider belonging in clans and herds, and coming together in large groups like this one is a source of tremendous joy and excitement.

Some have spent the morning splashing and soaking in a spring which they excavated and extended to make an (almost) elephant-sized pool. How elephants love to soak and wallow – you can almost hear the ahhh, the inner groan of pleasure as the muscles of the face relax and they let themselves slide into welcoming water and muddy ooze. It is touching and funny to watch: if the water is deep enough, even the most dignified adult will submerge completely, leaving the trunk to bob like a flexible periscope from the depths.

Now they're ready to play. One little female, very daring, strides over to our jeep, ears flaring boldly, and shoves the bonnet with her trunk. She's already strong enough to give the jeep a good shake. Chris cries out "hey" and gives the windshield a sharp rap, sending her running back to her family. She was playing at being big and brave, confronting possible enemies, just like the grown-ups do, and there is a comical expression of mingled delight, pride and alarm – "look what I just did!" – on her smooth, pretty face. The others don't seem concerned by her antics. Youngsters have to be allowed to explore and learn through their own experience, and while young males enjoy pushing and shoving contests, females get a thrill from chasing imaginary enemies.

It's different when a baby, maybe 6 months old, wanders in our direction. Mother or auntie hustles it away, the miniature trunk dangling like a jointed rubber hose. Babies are vulnerable. And that trunk is a great mystery to them at first, the way it bounces around, leading its own semi-independent life. It takes years for the young elephant to master the complex interplay of muscles and subtle sense perceptions that give the trunk its sensitivity and power. The adult can use her trunk to touch and smell. She can lift an egg without breaking it, or kill with a single blow. She can even sense the distant reverberations of thunder through her trunk; like the toes and feet, the elephant's trunk has special nerve endings that are sensitive to vibration and long-distance, low-frequency sound, passing through the air and ground.

Adults take their responsibilities seriously, but they also love to fool around. The science of animal behaviour takes a solemn view of play: officially, this is the way that young animals prepare for the serious work of adulthood. But elephants love play for its own sake. When times are good, the simple joy of being alive just wells up in them and pours out as fun and humour.

"Everyone says how smart they are" Vicky, a researcher who works with Joyce Poole in Amboseli, told writer Carl Safina. "But they can be ridiculous too. If a young male doesn't have a friend around, he'll make a little mock charge at us, then back up or twirl around. I actually had one male kneel down right in front of the car and throw zebra bones at me, trying to get me to play with him…. Sometimes they put bushes on their heads and just look at you like that. Ridiculous." (*Beyond Words. What Animals Think and Feel*. Carl Safina. 2015)

To our left, two young males are play-sparring, pushing and shoving with foreheads and trunks. They separate and the larger – known as Cheeky, according to Chris – walks away. There is a confident bounce to Cheeky's stride, his ears are wide, he looks like he's feeling good – then he pauses, seems to come to a sudden decision and heads towards our jeep, trunk swinging jauntily from side to side.

He moves silently on padded feet and halts in front. In his mid-twenties, not even fully-grown, Cheeky already towers over the bonnet. Chris whispers "Don't move now, don't make a sound." Cheeky considers us thoughtfully for a moment, then he dips his trunk, gathers up some sand and scatters it over his head and shoulders. He does it again and again, covering himself with dust, occasionally directing a trunkful towards the jeep so that it falls rattling on the bonnet and roof. There's nothing threatening: he's simply making sure that we really know that he's there.

When he feels that he has impressed us for long enough with his confidence and presence, he saunters off... pauses... points his trunk in our direction, widens the tip...and lifts it to his mouth. He's gathering our scents, I think.

And then I see another male stride out from the scrub bushes, head and back thickly coated with red dust. It's not Voortrekker, but an older male with the same sense of assured authority. Without making a sound that we can hear, he draws Cheeky and his friend over to him. Looking so much smaller as they stand before him, the two lift up their trunks and caress his head, his forehead, the side of his face, his jaw. The elder steps backwards into the bushes, but the younger ones can't bear to let him go. They follow, still caressing him, still embracing his head with their trunks, reaching out even further to lay their trunks across his shoulders.

It's the most fervent and devoted greeting I have ever seen, or imagined taking place between male animals.

Because males leave their birth family in early adolescence, researchers assumed they lived relatively solitary lives. More recently, scientists have discovered the depth of emotional connection between male elephants. US scientist Cathleen Rodham-O'Connell studies male social bonds at a waterhole in Etosha, in Northern Namibia. She calls it the buddy system. Male buddies, she writes, are not shy about their public displays of all-out affection for each other. One of the males in her study group, known as Greg, was extremely adept at keeping harmony in his mixed band of males, with their different ages and temperaments. Although he could be tough on signs of aggression, Greg was always gentle and patient with the young ones, especially those new to all-male society. "On one occasion we even witnessed him allowing a younger bull to suck on his tusks, a behaviour I had never seen before." she writes in *Elephant Don. The Politics of a Pachyderm Posse.*

Greg's nickname was "the Don" for the way his buddies always gave him a ritual trunk-to-mouth greeting when they met – which O'Connell jokingly compared to the ritual kissing of the Mafia Don's ring.

Strong male elders like Greg, who act as mentors for youngsters, also help them to manage the powerful hormone spikes that occur as they enter musth, the male sexual state, when testosterone levels can quadruple. Just like a teenage boy struggling with the confusing effects of puberty, young males must learn to cope with their new testosterone surges, and the aggressive urges they may cause. Like all teenagers, they need to test and temper their growing power in safe surroundings.

Males are much bigger than females, being twice as heavy and about a third taller, so it takes another male to keep a burly adolescent in check. This is where O'Connell's research gets really fascinating. She mapped the dung piles left by different males, collected and dried them and analysed the hormone levels. When she correlated them with behaviour she saw a clear pattern emerge. One belligerent teenager called Tyler, for example, experienced testosterone spikes, which dropped sharply every time Tyler received an emphatic shove or head butt from an older male. The elders were keeping these youngsters in balance, both emotionally and physically, by bringing their erratic adolescent hormones down to manageable levels.

When Cathleen Rodham-O'Connell tested for a relationship between social status in the male buddy group and high testosterone levels, she found none. On the contrary: high-status males maintained low levels of testosterone. They exercised leadership through insight and effective communication, not through displays of intimidation.

When I reflected afterwards on the tenderness of that elephant greeting ceremony, I felt that the elder was so rooted in his own being, that he could effortlessly draw the younger ones to him, and hold them within his presence in a way that was profoundly reassuring for them. In return, they offered him the expressions of their devotion, and their love.

To me the interaction seemed silent. But it is likely that unheard rumbles of reassurance were passing back and forth between them, because a large part of elephant vocal communication lies below the threshold of human hearing. Elephant voices span 10 octaves, from subsonic rumblings to great, brassy trumpet calls. Their low-frequency calls travel through the ground as well through the air, and can be received through specials cells in their feet as well as the ears.

The first scientist to become aware of the importance of elephant infrasound was Katie Payne. Payne, a musician, had previously discovered the beautiful and complex structures of humpback whales songs while working with Roger Payne. Standing by some captive elephants in a zoo she sensed a powerful, yet silent thrumming on the air. The resonance it set up in her body recalled the deepest bass notes of the organ, as it drops to the limits of the human ability to perceive vibration as sound. She called these unheard elephant sounds "Silent Thunder."

Among animals, only the largest – the blue whale, the fin whale and the elephant – drop into that infrasound range, as they send their voices on long-distant sound channels through earth, water and air. The other sources of long-range, low-frequency sound rise from the Earth itself – the shudder of earthquakes, volcanic eruptions, rolling thunder and great ocean storms, resonating over great distances.

'Silent Thunder' is a wonderful expression: it conveys the epic, majestic scale of elephant lives, as their voices resonate with the deep and constant powers of making that fashion the foundations of life on earth for all beings. Silent Thunder has another dimension for me as well. It reminds me of all the voices that we human cannot hear, since we closed our minds to their meaning and significance. The way we deafened ourselves to the thunder of other voices who share life with us on Earth.

First the western religious mind stripped soul and breath from other creatures and the Earth itself. As the scientific method took form, Rene Descartes described animals as "natural automata" without reason, language or even feeling. One of his followers, the philosopher Malebranche put it like this: "Animals eat without pleasure, cry without pain, grow without knowing it; they desire nothing, fear nothing, know nothing."

These ideas did not remain as philosophical abstractions: they were used to justify dreadful suffering, to dismiss as meaningless the cries of pain from dogs and other creatures during live dissections.

In the twentieth century, behavioural science maintained this rigid boundary between humans and other animals. Animals were seen as devoid of inner life, driven by simple, reflexive behaviours – survival, competition for food and mates, the evolutionary pressures of changing environments. They were biological machines "blindly programmed to preserve the selfish molecules known as genes" in the words of Richard Dawkins in *The Selfish Gene*.

What a terrible prison of the mind we made, when we confined consciousness to the particular form it has taken in the human, and denied it to other beings. And what liberation as a new understanding sweeps away these rigid ideas and frozen sense of separation. Scientists from many different disciplines – biologists, zoologists, evolutionary biologists, comparative psychologist, neuroscientists – state openly now that consciousness, in varying degrees of refinement and complexity, is not confined to the human, or even to the vertebrate brain.

Here is an extract from the 2012 Cambridge Declaration on Consciousness, made by a group of prominent neurologists and signed in the presence of physicist Stephen Hawking: "the weight of evidence indicates that humans are not unique in possessing the neurological substrates that generate consciousness. Non-human animals, including all mammals and birds, and many other creatures, including octopuses, also possess these neurological substrates."

Compare this with the words of a traditional Netsilik Eskimo, Nalunglaq, to the Danish ethnographer, Rasmussen: "In the very earliest times, when both people and animals lived on earth, a person could become an animal if he wanted to, and an animal could become a human being. Sometimes they were people, and sometimes animals and there was no difference. All spoke the same language."

It seems that the scientific and ancient shamanic worldviews may find common ground through renewed understanding of the continuity of consciousness and the interrelatedness and unity of all life.

I began to explore animal consciousness about 10 years ago, after meeting an African gray parrot living in New York who has a remarkable ability to use human language. N'kisi was about 5 years old at the time, which is young in parrot terms, but his human, Aimee, had already taught him a working vocabulary of several hundred words, which he combined in inventive ways to express himself. Primatologist Dr Jane Goodall had also been to meet N'kisi. Before she arrived, Aimee showed N'kisi a video of Dr Goodall among the chimpanzees of Gonbe. N'kisi's first words to her – said in a nasal New York accent – were "Gotta a chimp?"

Which was a pretty good opening line, showing that N'kisi had

a) recognized the real person from the memory of a moving image and b) understood her connection with an animal he had only seen on television. On the video taken of their meeting, the two chatter happily away together in a spontaneous duet of parrot and primatologist.

Not that long ago, most scientists would have scoffed at the idea that parrots could use human language to express themselves in a meaningful way. Birds, with their small brains, were thought to be missing key neural areas that make cognition possible. But Irene Pepperberg's work with another African gray parrot, Alex, demonstrated that Alex understood what he was saying, had a grasp of basic numbers, and could use human words to convey demanding abstract concepts, such as same/different and some/none.

Since then, researchers have found a remarkable variety of cognitive talents – problem solving and tool making – in ravens, crows and other birds. And new studies on other species keep on appearing, from the demonstration of empathy in rats to the subtle communication of insects, from syntax in dolphins to the very slime-moulds who have shown that, given time, they can work out the way out through a maze.

Laboratory work on captive animals can be overly academic. Sometimes researchers don't pay enough attention to the ways in which animals actually perceive the world; they forget that they are dealing with a quality of intelligence which is embodied and relational, not abstract and conceptual. In one experiment for example, it appeared that a captive elephant couldn't figure out how to use a stick held with the trunk to knock down a piece of suspended fruit. Then somebody realized that asking an elephant to reach for food while holding a stick with its trunk was pretty silly – because the stick was blocking their sense of smell, and confusing them. Give the elephant a stool, though, and he will immediately use it to stand on and reach for the fruit.

It's the same with the famous 'mirror tests' that are used to check for self-awareness in animals. We humans recognize our own image in the mirror around the age of three. So do a number of other animals, including chimpanzees. Some captive dolphins become so fascinated by their own image that they can examine themselves in a mirror for hours. (Which just goes to show how boring it must be for a dolphin to live inside a tank.)

It was thought that elephants lacked this critical sense of 'self-awareness' because they didn't seem to recognize their own mirror image. Until somebody examined the mirror from the elephant's perspective and realized they simply couldn't see themselves properly.

Rather than imposing human standards on other beings, real understanding comes, I think, through watching animals in the wild, behaving naturally, on their own terms. Captive elephants will cooperate and work together, motivated by the prospect of reward through food. That's interesting in the abstract. But it only becomes truly meaningful when the capacity for cooperation is illuminated by the love and care that elephants show for their offspring and one other.

Consider this story from the elephants of Amboseli in Kenya: Cynthia Moss once saw an elephant baby fall into a steep water hole. The mother and the baby's aunt could not reach down to lift the baby out. So they started digging out one side of the water hole and they dug until they had made a ramp which allowed the baby to clamber out.

Communication, co-operation, judgement and planning – these overlapping aspects of thought and feeling are united here, not through some external reward, but through the great love that lives in the hearts of these devoted beings.

Love and loss are inextricable. Love and loss and grief are interwoven in elephant lives, just as they are in our own. "An elephant can die of grief" writes Dame Daphne Sheldrick, a woman who knows their emotional depths better than almost anybody, having loved and raised many elephant orphans, lost some and returned many to the wild. "They grieve and mourn the loss of a loved one, just as deeply as we do and their capacity for love is humbling."

In Sunburu, Kenya, when a matriarch called Eleanor collapsed, another matriarch, Grace, quickly approached and managed to lift her and help her back on her feet. When Eleanor collapsed again, Grace stayed by her side that night until she died. Over the next week, Eleanor's family Grace and other friends came at various times and kept vigil by her body.

The companionship that elephants keep in dying extends to the body and bones of family and friends they have lost. Elephants respond deeply to a dead elephant's remains, even when all that is left are the bones. They gather around them in silence, and run their trunk tips with great delicacy over the teeth, the jaw, the bones of the skull, the tusks if they have not been taken by poachers. "It is their silence that is most unsettling. The only sound is the slow blowing of air out of their trunks as they investigate their dead companions." Joyce Poole writes. "It's as if even the birds have stopped singing."

What do they feel in that silence? Are they remembering the voice, the touch, the presence of the one who has died? Do their hearts burn with the pain of their loss? Do they ponder the great mystery of death, as we do when we stand by the grave of somebody we have lost? I can't say, and it would be wrong to speculate. But I can imagine standing by them and sharing their silence, sunk in my own contemplation of the bones of an elephant that I too had come to know, and to love.

In this time, elephants have become acquainted with death and grief in a way never known before through their long habitation of the earth. And they have become acquainted with fear in a way never known before. Once they outgrew their predators; after adolescence life held few real threats for them. In Roman times, elephants inhabited the whole of Africa, from the Mediterranean shores to the Cape. Elephant trails connected the continent; their presence was a great natural force shaping the landscape and ecology. By a thousand years ago, the demand for ivory, which rose in tandem with the slave trade, had eliminated them entirely from North Africa. In the 1800s an estimated 10 million elephants inhabited Africa; today there are fewer than 400,000 and their chance of dying at the hands of a human is greater than their risk of death from any other cause.

The demand for ivory has intensified to the point that almost no park or reserve is really large enough to allow them to live out their lives in peace and safety. Every year, another 30-35,000 elephants are slaughtered across Africa. That's almost 10 percent of the elephant population every year. Follow that curve on a graph and it tells you that in 15–20 years few will remain outside of fenced areas, little better than zoos, or the rare countries like Botswana which still have large and effectively-protected herds.

Sometimes I can't quite believe our inability to learn from experience: in 1990 a hard-won outright ban on the ivory trade almost put an end to poaching; ivory prices plummeted and ravaged elephant populations began to recover. Then a series of 'one-off' sales to China of stock-piled ivory from Namibia, Botswana, South Africa and Zimbabwe set the market aflame once more, and sent ivory prices soaring from $200 a pound in 2004 to more than $2000 a pound in 2013.

Namibia's small population of desert elephants is vulnerable in a different way. Although their tusks have little value as ivory because of the lack of certain minerals in their diet, the elephants themselves are sometimes sold as trophies to foreign hunters. A permit to hunt Voortrekker himself was issued a few years ago by the Namibian government. This remarkable being, with all his insight and experience, was reduced, like so many of his kin, to a mere commodity to be marketed and sold. He lived only because a group of dedicated people raised the money to buy the hunting permit and his life.

I hope that it is clear now that the loss of so many elephant lives means more than numbers, or population size, or calculations of what percentage of the species might be sufficient to ensure their survival. That is an outdated way to think. This crisis is about the shattering of communities and the ravaging of the elephant psyche. When the poachers have passed, and the bodies of slaughtered elephants are slowly turning to dust, grief and fear remain, etched deeply into elephant memories and minds. Some researchers, such as psychologist Gay Bradshow, tell us that elephants who survive violence and the traumatic break-up of their families suffer, as we humans do, from post-traumatic stress. They show similar emotional scars – they become depressed and lethargic, find it difficult to make decisions, are easily startled, and become prone to unpredictable outbreaks of violence.

The Universe, and in particular the planet Earth, is a communion of subjects, and not a collection of objects. If we don't understand that, nothing is going to work.
— Thomas Berry.

At night in Namibia, as the veil of daylight fades, the great river of stars appears, pouring across the southern sky, from horizon to horizon. Without the distraction of artificial light, you look up to the edge of the galaxy, burning across the night. The ordinary mind dissolves into a trance of wonder as you begin to glimpse the measureless depths of the universe.

The universe, surely, is more than burning matter. It has brought forth consciousness in a myriad forms, of which the human is simply one. Like the mythical Narcissus gazing obsessively at his image, captured in one small pool, we humans became so entranced by our own reflection, we forgot the depth and magnificence of the life we share with countless other beings.

When you are really present among wild creatures, there are times when they reveal themselves. They are no longer merely objects of the curious human gaze, but fellow subjects. You glimpse their deeper being, and the beauty and mystery that inhabit them, showing through the physical form. And in those moments of communion, the wound of our human exile from the unity of the living world can, finally, be healed.

* * *

Editor's Note:

A list of references for this chapter and some relevant links can be found on this book's companion Web page at www.greenspirit-ebooks.info.

Eleanor O'Hanlon is an author and conservationist who has carried out field research for international conservation and wildlife groups. Her articles on wildlife, wilderness and animal behaviour have appeared in BBC Wildlife, Geo, Animan, the Dark Mountain Project and others. Her first book *Eyes of the Wild Journeys of Transformation with the Animal Powers* explores the ancient, shamanic understanding of animals as guides to the awakening of the soul in a series of journeys with whales, wolves, bears and wild horses. It was awarded the 2014 Nautilus Gold Book Award for Nature Writing. Eleanor is currently at work on a second book.

CONCLUSION

As I said, right at the beginning of this book, you may be surrounded by other people – friends, family, neighbours and acquaintances – who are also quite 'green' in their ideas and habits. Or you may not be. If you are not, you are probably keenly aware of it and wish you had more like-minded people around you. And it is likely that these are the people you enjoy meeting and sharing ideas and experiences with. These are among the relationships that you find most precious. And if this final chapter has resonated with you, it is very likely that your relationships with the more-than-human world are also precious to you.

We all need a support system, especially in these troubled times. Once you fully understand that the entire planet and all its elements are part of that support system and that all lives are interwoven and interdependent and, more importantly, once you have reached the point where that understanding is what informs your life on a daily basis, you are practising deep green living. Your lifestyle and your spirituality match.

But how did you reach that point? Where did you get your inspiration and guidance? And which came first: a green spirituality or a desire to live sustainably? Some years ago, I tried asking this question of a number of people.

Their answers varied. One said: "I started simplifying my life by decluttering and downshifting to make life easier. As I went through this process and joined discussion groups, the spiritual aspect gradually became more important and now looking after our world is very important to me. This means using public transport or walking as much as possible, buying only essential items and then second-hand if possible, wearing my clothes until they are worn out and buying food locally. I have found these changes very enriching and am much happier since adopting this lifestyle."

Another said something very similar. For her, too, the desire for simplicity was the first step. She wanted "less clutter, less confusion and clear priorities." But as she explained: "…this seemed to lead naturally to deeper thoughts, and then expanding my at first 'selfish' impulse to thoughts about how I affected the world. I read things like Jane Goodall's Harvest for Hope and Barbara Kingsolver's Animal, Vegetable, Miracle. Both had the message that we can make good choices about what we consume, not just food but resources to create or transport that food, and even the attitudes we choose to absorb or reject. Reflecting on and being in the natural world seems to underlie my desire to be more conscious, more connected to what is 'real' in the world."

Sometimes, a love of Nature came first. One respondent explained that she had grown up in a family of gardeners, campers and hikers. Nature was a huge part of her life. The natural world had always spoken to her deeply and nurtured her. "The serenity of sitting by the lake, the majesty of the mountains, lying in the grass looking at the stars and knowing that life is about more than just me creates a longing to better care for the Earth. And I was taught to always leave a place better than when you found it." So for her, downshifting in the area of work and gave her the time to celebrate the coming of a New Moon, harvesting and the changing of the seasons. "I am filled with gratitude for the world as it is," she said "…and desire to keep doing my part in sustaining the Earth."

Sometimes, the answer to 'which came first for you, simplicity or spirituality?' had an unexpected answer. One person told me that what had come first for her was in fact fear. "Listening to Al Gore's presentation of an 'An Inconvenient Truth' two and a half years ago, and seeing his exponential chart of rising CO2 with the red dents spiking is all it took to transform me from a 'couldn't care less about the environment' into a determined 'will do all I can to help' person." As a result, she turned to blogging and that, she said, "... took me into places I had not foreseen, of Zen and deep connection with other human beings, and Nature." She told me that she sees the current planetary emergency as the result of a spiritual void to begin with. "Our insatiable desire for always more things to do, to buy, and to possess, strikes me as a manifestation of the emptiness we feel, collectively. The mall has become our new church, and place of worship."

One man replied that downshifting to both a more low impact and a simpler lifestyle hasn't so much changed his spiritual outlook as allowed it to bloom fully. "My life was pot bound for many years. I was a workaholic who never switched off, drank too much and got through a box of painkillers a week. Yet I had always had both green and spiritual and (if I can use the work both affectionately and proudly) 'hippy' tendencies. These qualities were submerged to the demands and sacrifices of corporate life. They were all relegated as mere hobbies, frippery and cosy fantasies of self-sufficiency in a future I accepted, on some level, that would never be fully realised." But in searching for a way to alleviate severe back pain, he learned meditation and through that he was led to Buddhism. From there, his greenness and his spirituality arose together. "The greenness could not be what it is without the gentle force of Buddhism behind it. Likewise, I could not conceive of a Buddhist outlook in which ecology is not important. But moreover it was all there in me already, waiting to arise with its own flavour in me when it had the space to do so. All the conditions needed to be there for it to become manifest. Voluntary simplicity made the space for all that to happen."

No matter which way they answered, every one of my respondents agreed that regardless of which aspect of their lives had risen to importance first, the other followed automatically. And now, both were equally important to them.

Obviously, those people whose spirituality has always been green are going to be people who try their hardest to care for the Earth and to keep their eco-footprints as low as they can. But also it seems to me that those who for one reason or another downshift to a simpler, more sustainable lifestyle almost always come to a much deeper appreciation of Nature, the seasons, their own bodies and in fact of life itself. The greener you are, the greener you get.

But like the people I have quoted here, for many of us the journey begins from a sense of dissatisfaction with the 'standard' way of living in our mechanistic, techno-dazzled, industrialized, over-working, consumerist society. And our first steps towards change can be tentative and perhaps shaky.

From where, then, can we get inspiration, encouragement and guidance to keep us going along what can sometimes be a lonely and difficult path?

Nowadays, since issues like climate change and peak oil have emerged into public awareness, some religious leaders are now exhorting their congregations to do more towards caring for the planet and to downshift to more environmentally conscious lifestyles. Sad to say, a lot of the blame for the pickle our planet is in can be placed at the door of organized religion, with its historical attempts to prise humans out of their deep embeddedness in the natural world and interest them, instead, in promises of eternal life in some other dimension. But let's just be glad that the churches are finally starting to encourage greenness, even though their sermons, just like most secular sermons about 'the environment', are largely if not wholly motivated by self-interest. We must save the forests (so that we can breathe oxygen), protect the oceans (so that we can go on eating fish) conserve resources (so that we can eke out what's left of the oil), downshift (so that we don't all finish up starving to death because there are too many of us and not enough food to go round) and so on. It is always all about us. And sometimes, as an afterthought, the other species with whom we share the planet. After all, if we let them all die out, then we wouldn't have those fascinating Nature programs to watch on TV any more, would we? (Oops, I am sounding cynical.)

Self-interest has always been a good motivator. But, as we have already discussed, it is not always easy to join the dots and to make connections between an action we take today and our wellbeing – or someone else's wellbeing – in the future, or even in the present.

The deepest, strongest and most meaningful and enduring motivation is the spiritual one. Put quite simply: we are the planet. What we do to Her, we do to ourselves. When we truly love the Earth we walk on, when we respect and have reverence for every other life form, when we really get it that every being has intrinsic value and everything is sacred, then everything else falls into place. That's when downshifting becomes as natural – and as vitally important to us – as breathing. In our love of Gaia, that is where we can find the inspiration and the guidance that we are seeking.

However, it is all very well in theory. It's easy to love the Earth on a bright and sunny morning and when things are going well. It's easy to love a fluffy kitten or a cute little wren, the perfection of a snowflake, the splendour of a rainbow over the mountains.
But can you feel equally kindly towards the sparrowhawk that swoops down and snatches the wren? Can you love a virus? Can you have reverence for an earthquake? A tsunami?

We know that the ideal is to love others – especially our partners and our children – unconditionally, but sometimes it is hard. How much harder to love a planet that as well as awesomely beautiful can also be awesomely destructive, unspeakably harsh. And despite how prettily the stars twinkle in the night sky, how much harder still it is to love the vast and measureless universe in which that planet floats. A universe in which our own significance shrinks to zero and one whose origins remain shrouded in a mystery that is utterly incomprehensible to our puny, human minds. Thinking about that can soon make us fearful and contracted.

At a psychic level most of us spend our whole lives in this contracted state. Fear makes us cautious. The lack of certainty terrifies us. The possibility of calamity narrows our vision. It makes us shrivel up, huddle into ourselves, vainly seeking comfort by curling up in a ball, like a hedgehog, rather than remaining fully open to everything that is around us and open to all the uncertainties of the next moment.

Most of us are afraid, most of the time, though often not consciously so. We fear illness, we fear death, we fear the unknown future. The great mystery that is life scares most of us rigid. So we snuggle desperately into the familiar – into our relationships, our work, our routines, our library books and movies: always seeking comfort. I've heard it called existential angst. Just to be alive is scary if you let yourself really face life – and death – full-on.

So most of us, most of the time, distract ourselves from existential angst and our deep-seated fear of the unknown and what might happen in our personal – or planetary – future. We attempt to insulate ourselves in any way we can think of. Like seeking certainty where there really is none by following, blindly, the precepts and prescriptions of off-the-peg belief systems. In the same way that we seal up cracks in our houses so that no cold draught may enter, we fill up all the spaces in our consciousness into which fear may possibly creep. Thus we go shopping for things we don't really need, put iPods in our ears, jabber and text on our cell phones, stay busy with our computers, our social lives, our work, the TV…anything to stop ourselves from thinking too hard about all the unknowns that scare us and all the question marks hanging over us as individuals and as members of what may well be a doomed species.

The truth is that no matter how much we try to kid ourselves, there are no guarantees, no escapes and no safe places. I think that is what Christ meant when he said "The foxes have holes and the birds of the air have nests, but the Son of Man hath not where to lay His head" (Matthew 8:20). We humans are stuck with our existential dilemma: the dilemma of knowing enough to be scared but not enough to comforted. We cannot unravel the Great Mystery. All we can do is take a deep breath, step forward and breathe "yes" to it.

Saying "yes" to everything, including the possibility of annihilation and the loss of all that we hold dear, from robins to eagles to ourselves and to all illusions of security and certainty, is the only true course open to us. Opening up to whatever may happen, opening up to the unknown future, saying "yes" to life – no matter what – is, I believe, the ultimate spiritual challenge. This step is not for sissies. It is a lot like striding confidently down an icy hill on a winter morning, looking up and out at the world instead of creeping along, staring anxiously down at one's boots. But only after we have accepted all the possibilities can we stride confidently into action. Only when we have faced the worst that might happen to us and to our world can we work tirelessly to create the peaceful, abundant, green world of which we dream. Courage is not about the denial of fear. It is about facing the fear and moving through it and beyond it. That is where we find our guidance, our inspiration and a wellspring of spiritual energy. And when we seek comfort, we can find it by learning to let go of our sense of individual importance and remembering that since we are part of the planet we shall never disappear. Our sense of separateness was only ever a temporary illusion. Just as every wave is simply part of the ocean, we are each part of a greater whole. For Gaia is us and we are Gaia and there is no death, only constant change and transformation.

So that, I believe, is the deepest, greenest thing we can possibly do: saying "yes" to life, acknowledging that walking our talk to the

very best of our ability is all that is required of us. And then...
letting go – and letting Gaia.

*   *   *

FURTHER
RESOURCES AND
EDITOR'S NOTE

FURTHER RESOURCES

This book has a companion website (www.greenspirit-ebooks. info) which is kept fully updated. There you will find:

- links to the websites of this book's editor and some of its contributors

- a link to the main GreenSpirit website which in turn has a large resource section and links to many other relevant websites

- details of the other books in this series and where to get them

- a blog, where you can leave your comments about this and other books in the series, read what others have to say about the books, ask questions about green spirituality and share the blog posts you like on Facebook, Twitter etc.

- announcements about forthcoming books and other GreenSpirit news

* * *

GreenSpirit magazine

"For many of us, it's the spirit running through that limitless span of green organisations and ideas that anchors all the work we do. And 'GreenSpirit' is an invaluable source of insight, information and inspiration."
—JONATHON PORRITT.

EDITOR'S NOTE

I hope you have enjoyed reading this little book as much as I have enjoyed editing it. And I give my heartfelt thanks to all who have contributed to its pages. This is the sixth volume in an ongoing series of books about the many and varied ways in which green spirituality can be expressed in every aspect of our lives and culture and we hope many more volumes will be added to the series in the coming years.

If you like this – or any of our other GreenSpirit book – please consider taking a few moments to leave a little review on your favourite online retailer's website and/or post something about it on a site such as Facebook.

Blessings to all,
Marian

Other GreenSpirit books

GreenSpirit
Path to a New Consciousness
Edited by Marian Van Eyk McCain

Published by Earth Books
ISBN 978-1-84694-290-7

Meditations with Thomas Berry
With additional material
by Brian Swimme
Selected by June Raymond

Published by GreenSpirit
ISBN 978-0-9552157-4-2

Other titles in the GreenSpirit book series

What is Green Spirituality?
Edited by Marian Van Eyk McCain

All Our Relations: GreenSpirit Connections with the More-than-Human World
Edited by Marian Van Eyk McCain

The Universe Story in Science and Myth
Greg Morter and Niamh Brennan

Rivers of Green Wisdom: Exploring Christian and Yogic Earth Centred Spirituality
Santoshan (Stephen Wollaston)

Pathways of Green Wisdom: Discovering Earth Centred Teachings in Spiritual and Religious Traditions
Edited by Santoshan (Stephen Wollaston)

Free for members ebook editions

32841084R00095

Printed in Great Britain
by Amazon